Hypr

Hypnosis for Deep Sleep

Powerful Guided Meditation to Quiet Your Mind.

How to Improve Your Sleep Quality and Fall Asleep Instantly Every Night Without Anxiety and Stress

Hypnosis for Deep Sleep

Table of Contents

CHAPTER 1. WHY SHOULD I SLEEP BETTER? 8
- WHY DO WE NEED TO SLEEP? 8
- HOW DOES SLEEP WORK? 9
- BENEFITS OF SLEEPING WELL 16
- DISADVANTAGES OF LITTLE AND BAD SLEEP 20
- THE MAIN CAUSES BECAUSE I CAN'T FALL ASLEEP AND SLEEP WELL 31

CHAPTER 2. HOW TO SOLVE THE PROBLEMS OF INSOMNIA WITHOUT MEDICINE? 43
- WHAT IS INSOMNIA? 43
- DON'T BE A HERO: THE HARMFUL EFFECTS OF INSOMNIA 43
- SLEEP HYGIENE 45
- WHAT IS COGNITIVE-BEHAVIORAL THERAPY FOR INSOMNIA? 49
- BEST REMEDIES 54

CHAPTER 3. FOODS FOR BETTER SLEEP 61
- WHAT SHOULD YOUR SLEEP DIET LOOK LIKE? 61
- IS THERE ANY FOOD TO KEEP YOU AWAKE? 62
- SHOULD I EAT AND DRINK BEFORE GOING TO BED? 62
- DAY DIET FOR A NIGHT'S SLEEPING WELL 72
- FOODS TO AVOID BEFORE GOING TO BED 77
- ADEQUATE SLEEPING POSTURES 82
- THE BEST SLEEPING POSTURE FOR SLEEP APNEA AND SNORING 88
- BEST SLEEPING POSITIONS DURING PREGNANCY 90
- THE BEST SLEEPING POSITION FOR BACK PAIN 93
- BABY SLEEPING POSITION 97

CHAPTER 4. CREATE AN IDEAL SLEEPING ENVIRONMENT 104
- ORGANIZE THE ROOM 104
- CREATE A PERFECT SLEEPING ENVIRONMENT FOR YOUR BABY 114
- HEALTHY HABITS, LET YOU SLEEP WELL 116
- BETTER SLEEP HABITS 119

CHAPTER 5. POSITIVE AFFIRMATIONS FOR BETTER SLEEP ... 131
- AFFIRMATION FOR RELIVE ANXIETY 141
- AFFIRMATION TO HELP YOU FIND HAPPINESS 155

CHAPTER 6. WHAT IS HYPNOSIS 169

HYPNOSIS AND SLEEP 172
SLEEP HYPNOSIS SCIENCE 176
WHAT IS SLEEP HYPNOSIS? 177
DOES IT WORK? 178
EVIDENCE OF SELF-HYPNOSIS DURING SLEEP 179
IS SLEEPING EFFECTIVELY DURING HYPNOSIS? 182
WHAT IS MEDITATION SLEEP? 183
WHAT MAKES PEOPLE GET UP AT NIGHT? 183
BENEFITS OF SLEEP MEDITATION 184
GUIDED SLEEP MEDITATION TECHNIQUES 185
TEN-STEP MEDITATION PRACTICE TO IMPROVE SLEEP 187
WHY SHOULD I TRY TO FALL ASLEEP? 192
DEEP SLEEP MEDITATION TECHNIQUES 194

CHAPTER 7. VISUALIZE YOUR PATH THROUGH MEDITATION 200

YOUR VISION AND GOALS 201
WHY MEDITATION AND VISUALIZATION ARE NOT THE SAME AND HOW TO USE THEM 202
MEDITATION STEPS FOR ACHIEVING YOUR GOALS 204
HYPNOSIS TO IMPROVE SLEEP QUALITY AND FALL ASLEEP INSTANTLY 211
WHAT IF I CANNOT SLEEP? 213
HYPNOSIS TO FALL ASLEEP 215

CONCLUSION 218

RACHEL ERIKSON

© Copyright 2020 - All rights reserved.

The content contained within this book may not be reproduced, duplicated or transmitted without direct written permission from the author or the publisher.

Under no circumstances will any blame or legal responsibility be held against the publisher, or author, for any damages, reparation, or monetary loss due to the information contained within this book. Either directly or indirectly.

Legal Notice:

This book is copyright protected. This book is only for personal use. You cannot amend, distribute, sell, use, quote or paraphrase any part, or the content within this book, without the consent of the author or publisher.

Disclaimer Notice:

Please note the information contained within this document is for educational and entertainment purposes only. All effort has been executed to present accurate, up to date, and reliable, complete information. No warranties of any kind are declared or implied. Readers acknowledge that the author is not engaging in the rendering of legal, financial, medical or professional advice. The content within this book has been derived from various sources. Please consult a licensed professional before attempting any techniques outlined in this book.

By reading this document, the reader agrees that under no circumstances is the author responsible for any losses, direct or indirect, which are incurred as a result of the use of information contained within this document, including, but not limited to, — errors, omissions, or inaccuracies.

Chapter 1. Why Should I Sleep Better?

Adequate sleep is essential to help a person maintain optimal health and happiness. As far as their health is concerned, sleep, regular exercise, and a balanced diet are crucial. In the United States and many other countries, modern life does not always include the need for adequate sleep. However, people must strive to get enough sleep regularly. Here are the many benefits associated with a good night's sleep for health professionals. Lack of sleep at night will make you lose your temper the next day. Over time, lack of sleep may not only mess up your morning mood. Studies have shown that regular quality sleep can help improve everything from blood sugar to exercise.

Why Do We Need to Sleep?

When sleeping, it is difficult for the body to clean up the mess during the day. Your system is busy removing toxins, replacing cells, repairing damaged tissues, and restoring energy supply. Sleep gives you time to heal and recover so that you can rest the next day. Insufficient sleep can lead to a lack of sleep, which can have long-term effects on your health, including the danger of diabetes, heart disease, obesity, and depression.

How Does Sleep Work?

Once you go to the cafe to start your day, your body is already preparing for sleep. When you are awake, your body produces a chemical called adenosine, which accumulates throughout the day and eventually causes drowsiness, indicating that you are ready to go to bed. Your sleep and daily relationship with wakefulness are controlled by two systems: your biological clock (or circadian rhythm) and sleep motivation. Your circadian rhythm is a biochemical cycle that repeats approximately every 24 hours and controls sleep, wake-up time, hunger, body temperature, hormone release, and other rhythms closely related to the 24-hour working day. The sleeping driver (need to sleep) will determine the amount of sleep and intensity of sleep required based on how long you are awake. Think about your sleep drive like hunger; it will build throughout the day until it is satisfied. Here are some points:

Higher Productivity and Concentration

Several studies conducted by scientists in the early 2000s looked at the effects of sleep deprivation. The researchers concluded that sleep is related to multiple brain functions, including:

- Concentration

- Productivity

- Understanding

Reduced Risk of Weight Gain

The connection between weight gain and obesity and short sleep patterns is not fully understood. Over the years, several studies have linked obesity with poor sleep patterns. However, a new study in the Journal Sleep Medicine concluded no link between being overweight and sleep deprivation. After you rest, you won't be so hungry. Lack of sleep destroys leptin and growth hormone-releasing in the brain, thereby controlling appetite. With these imbalances, your resistance to the temptation of unhealthy foods will be significantly reduced.

Moreover, when you are tired, you are unlikely to want to move your body. In short, this is the secret to gaining weight. The time you spend in bed is closely related to the time you spend at the table and the gym to help you control your weight.

This study believes that many previous studies failed to consider other factors, such as:

- Drinking
- Have type 2 diabetes
- Physical activity level
- Education level

- Long work time

- Sedentary time

Insufficient sleep may affect a person's desire or ability to maintain a healthy lifestyle. Still, it may or may not be a direct cause of weight gain.

Better Calorie Regulation

Like gaining weight, there is evidence that good sleep can help a person consume fewer calories during the day. For example, a study stated that sleep patterns affect the hormones that cause appetite. If a person does not sleep great enough, it may interfere with their body's ability to regulate food intake properly.

Higher Athletic Performance

An adult's adequate sleep time is 7 to 9 hours per night, and athletes may benefit from up to 10 hours. Therefore, sleep is as essential for athletes as consuming enough calories and nutrition. One of the reasons for this condition is that the body improves during rest. If your exercise requires rapid energy bursts (such as wrestling or weightlifting), then lack of sleep may not affect you as severely as endurance sports such as running, swimming, and cycling. But you did not help yourself. In addition to wasting energy and time to repair muscles, lack of sleep can also weaken your motivation, which is what brings you to an end. You will face even more daunting mental and physical challenges—and see slower reaction times.

Other benefits include:

- Better performance intensity
- Extra energy
- More careful coordination
- More active speed
- Better mental function

More Social and Emotional Intelligence

Sleep is related to people's emotional and social intelligence. People who don't get full sleep are more likely to have problems recognizing others' emotions and expressions. For example, a study in the Journal of Sleep Research looked at people's responses to emotional stimuli. Like many earlier studies, the researchers concluded that when a person does not get enough sleep, their emotional resonance will decrease.

Healthy Body

When you fall asleep, your body takes time to rest, recover, and rebuild to perform well the next day. By repairing damaged cells, strengthening the immune system, and replenishing energy for the heart and cardiovascular system the next day, your body will get a feeling of restarting, which can wake you up, refresh you, and provide alerts for daily activities. If you neglect your sleep plan and start to increase sleep deprivation, it may begin to cause severe damage to your body system. It may lead to chronic diseases such as diabetes, cardiovascular disease, Alzheimer's disease, and even cancer.

Lack of sleep can also significantly affect the body's small units, the immune system. The immune system is the body's defense mechanism, protecting you from foreign invaders trying to divide and conquer. Without proper sleep, your immune system may become weak, and it is difficult to defend against invaders. It may cause you to get sick more frequently and experience a slower recovery time when you recover.

When you forget to count those sheep every night, your circadian rhythms will become out of sync and begin to damage your hormone levels. Hormones regulate everything from the menstrual cycle to hunger. For example, when your body lacks sleep, it may destroy your body's ability to know when to be satisfied. When you don't get enough sleep, the hormones that make you feel full or hungry (leptin and ghrelin, respectively) may be out of balance, making you hungry. Sleep also affects insulin, a hormone in the body responsible for controlling blood sugar levels. If that is not enough, the hormones that regulate fertility can affect your ability to have children.

Sleep Improves Your Immune Function

Studies have shown that a short amount of sleep deprivation can weaken immune function. A sizeable 2-week study monitored the occurrence of the common cold after nasal drops of a cold virus. They found that people who slept for less than 7 hours were almost three times more likely to get a cold than those who slept for 8 hours. If you have frequent colds, it may help ensure at least 8 hours of sleep every night. Eating more garlic can also help.

Sharp Brain

When your sleep is insufficient, you may have difficulty keeping and recalling details. That's because rest performs a significant role in learning and memory. Without enough sleep, it isn't easy to concentrate on acquiring new information. Your brain also does not have enough time to store the memory correctly to extract it later.

Mood Enhancement

Another thing the brain does during sleep is to process emotions. Your mind needs this time to recognize and react correctly. When you shorten the time, there tend to be more negative emotional reactions and fewer positive reactions. Long-term lack of sleep can also increase the chance of suffering from mood disorders. A large study showed that people with insomnia are five times more likely to suffer from depression and have more significant anxiety or panic disorder. A refreshing sleep can help you press the reset button on bad days, improve your outlook on life, and be fully prepared for challenges.

Healthier Heart

When you sleep, your blood pressure drops, restoring your heart and blood vessels. The short you sleep, the longer your blood pressure stays in 24 hours. High blood pressure can cause heart disease, including stroke.

Stabilize Blood Sugar

During the deep, slow-wave part of the sleep cycle, the amount of glucose in the blood drops. There is not enough time at the deepest stage, which means you can't rest for a reset-like turning up the volume. Your body will have difficulty adapting to the demands of cells and blood sugar levels.

Bacteria Fight

To help you fight with the disease, your immune system recognizes harmful bacteria and viruses in your body and destroys them. Constant lack of sleep can change the way immune cells work. They may not attack so quickly, and you may get sicker. A good night's rest can now help you avoid that tired, exhausted feeling, and you can rest in bed for a few days while your body is trying to recover.

Benefits of Sleeping Well

In the past, sleep was often ignored by doctors and surrounded by myths. But now, we are beginning to understand the importance of sleep for overall health and well-being. For example, we learned that when people sleep less than 6 to 7 hours a night, they are at greater risk of disease. Are there more reasons to fall asleep? Here are some reasons why you should call it "late night."

Sleep Keeps Your Heart Healthy

Heart disease and stroke are more likely to occur in the early morning, which may be due to how sleep interacts with blood vessels. Lack of sleep is related to elevated blood pressure and cholesterol, the latter being risk factors for heart disease and stroke. If you sleep 7-9 hours a night, your heart will be healthier.

Sleep May Help Prevent Cancer

Did you know that people who work late at night have a higher risk of breast and colon cancer? Researchers believe that light will reduce the content of melatonin. Melatonin is a hormone that regulates the sleep-wake cycle. Because it can inhibit the growth of tumors, it is believed to prevent cancer. Ensure your bedroom is dark and avoid using electronic devices before going to bed to help your body produce the melatonin it needs.

Sleep Reduces Stress

When your body does not get enough sleep, it enters a state of stress. The body's functions are in a state of high alert, leading to high blood pressure and stress hormones. High blood pressure increases your risk of heart disease and stroke, and stress hormones make it difficult to fall asleep. Learn relaxation techniques to counteract the effects of stress and fall asleep faster.

Sleep Reduces Inflammation

The increase in stress hormones caused by lack of sleep increases the level of inflammation in the body. It increases the risk of heart disease, cancer, and diabetes. It is believed that inflammation will cause the body to deteriorate with age.

Sleep Makes You More Alert

A good night's sleep will keep you energized and alert the next day. Being engaged and active not only feels great, but it also increases your chances of getting a good night's sleep. When you wake up feeling refreshed, please use this energy to get into the sun, do some active things, and interact with your world. You will sleep better the next night and increase your daily energy level.

Sleep Improves Your Memory

Researchers do not fully understand why we fall asleep and dream, but they found that sleep plays a vital role in memory consolidation. Between events, sensory input, feelings, and memories. Deep sleep is essential for your brain to remember and make connections, and getting more quality sleep will help you remember and process things better.

Sleep Can Help You Lose Weight

Researchers have found that people who sleep less every night are more likely to be overweight or obese. It is believed that lack of sleep affects the balance of hormones in the body that affect appetite. It has been found that the hormones ghrelin and leptin, which regulate appetite, are interrupted by lack of sleep. If you want to maintain or lose weight, don't forget that getting enough sleep regular is an essential part of it.

Taking a Nap Makes You Smarter

The night is not the only time to capture anything. Pepping during the day is a practical, refreshing alternative to caffeine, which is good for your overall health and can increase your productivity. In one study, people who did not take a nap or who did not rest for less than one hour experienced an intellectual decline that was four to six times greater than those who took a nap for at least one hour. People who hit snooze at work show much lower pressure. Taking a nap can also improve memory, cognitive function, and mood.

Sleep Can Reduce the Risk of Depression

Sleep affects many chemicals in your body, including serotonin. People with serotonin deficiency are more likely to suffer from depression. By ensuring you get the right amount of sleep (7 to 9 hours per night), you can help prevent depression.

Sleep Helps the Body Repair Itself

Sleep is a time for relaxation, but it is also a time for the body to work hard to repair the damage caused by stress, UV rays, and other harmful exposures. Your cells produce more protein during sleep. These protein molecules form the building blocks of cells, enabling them to repair the damage.

Disadvantages of Little and Bad Sleep

If you have lacked sleep, it may cause serious health risks. In the short term, staying awake for 17 to 19 hours continuous may impair your reaction time. The blood alcohol content is 0.05%, which is legally considered drunk. Long-term lack of sleep may also increase your possibility of heart disease or mental illness. Here are some ways that lack of sleep can negatively affect your health:

Damage Your Mental Health

Lack of sleep can affect your mood and increase stress levels. Patients with insomnia are 17 times more likely to develop clinical anxiety compared to people without sleep deprivation. Non-depressed patients with insomnia are twice as likely to suffer from depression as people who sleep well. It may be due to the impact of lack of sleep on the brain's ability to regulate emotions, leading to emotional disturbances and negative thinking. For example, one study examined healthy participants who were deprived of sleep for 35 hours. When the sleep-deprived patients showed negative images, the amygdala (the brain area that regulates mood and anxiety levels) was more active than participants without sleep deprivation. Also, studies have found that 65% to 90% of adults with depression have sleep problems. Although lack of sleep can affect your mental health, depression can also cause insomnia, leading to a vicious circle.

Reduce Memory and Learning Ability

Researchers found that losing only five hours of sleep within 24 hours can cut the connections between hippocampal neurons and memory. Researchers found that among participants who slept during this time, the cerebellum is the brain area that controls accuracy. It shows that during sleep, memories are transferred to more efficient storage areas in the brain. Insufficient sleep may also impair the brain's ability to clear beta-amyloid, a toxic protein in the fluid between brain cells, and is associated with memory loss and Alzheimer's disease.

Make Weight Loss More Difficult

Sleeping less than seven to eight hours at night activates the body's endocannabinoid (ECB) system, which increases your appetite for pleasant but unhealthy foods such as candies and French fries. In a small study of 14 healthy young people, researchers found that participants who did not sleep for four nights had higher afternoon ECB levels than participants who had a good night's sleep. Elevated ECB levels increase their appetite and cravings for snacks. "It can increase the desire to eat by changing the normal release and levels of different hormones that cause hunger and satiety." The study also found that lack of sleep increases ghrelin (a hormone that stimulates appetite). And reduce the release of leptin (a hormone that makes you feel full). Also, if you don't get enough sleep, you may feel tired and don't have enough energy for regular exercise, leading to weight gain.

Increased Risk of Heart Disease

Regardless of your age, weight, whether you smoke or exercise, getting less than seven hours of sleep each night will increase your heart disease risk, heart attack, or stroke. Hypertension or high blood pressure is one of the main risk factors for heart disease. When you sleep well, your blood pressure should drop by about 10% to 20%, called night immersion. However, if you don't get the sleep you need, your blood pressure won't drop at night—studies have found that even a small increase in your night blood pressure level can lead to an increased risk of heart disease. Continuous lack of sleep can also affect the body's ability to regulate stress hormones, and long-term stress may cause heart attacks.

Cause Harmful Accidents

In 2017, in the United States, nine-car accidents reported by the police involved sleepy drivers—about 50,000 people were injured, and nearly 800 people were killed. Drowsy driving is similar to driving under the influence of banned substances. It slows down your reaction time and awareness of danger. It reduces your ability to pay attention to what you are doing. A study showed that drivers who slept for less than four hours in the first 24 hours were 15.1 times more likely to have a car accident than drivers who slept for 7 to 9 hours at the same time. Many work-related accidents are also attributed to a lack of sleep. Compared with workers with insufficient sleep, workers with inadequate sleep are 70% more likely to have an accident at work, and the probability of death from an accident is twice as high.

Lead to Poor Judgment

Lack of sleep can also lead to poor judgment. It may be because a lack of sleep affects the prefrontal cortex (the area that controls the brain's logical thinking). Examples include:

- People with insufficient sleep are more likely to take risks. In a study, participants can choose to receive a certain amount of money or desire to gamble to get more money, but they get nothing if they lose. People who sleep less than five hours a week are more likely to gamble than those who sleep eight hours.

- Lack of sleep can make you more impulsive. Studies have found that this makes people with insufficient sleep more

- likely to engage in aggressive behavior or lack self-control.

- Insufficient sleep can also affect your moral judgment because it impairs the brain's ability to use emotions and cognition to help you make decisions.

- Lack of sleep can obscure the moral decision-making process. For example, military personnel in combat may make choices, and if they take a good rest, they will not make choices such as hurting or killing someone to save others' lives.

- People who lack sleep may cheat more. The study also found that participants who slept 22 minutes less than other participants the night before were more likely to cheat to win raffle tickets.

Central Nervous System

The Central Nervous System is the leading information highway of the human body. Sleep is essential to keep functioning correctly, but chronic insomnia can disrupt your body's typically and processes information. During sleep, nerve cells (neurons) form pathways that help you remember new information you have learned. Insufficient sleep can exhaust your brain and, therefore, cannot perform its duties. You may also find it more difficult to concentrate or learn new things. Signals from your body may also be delayed, reducing coordination and increasing the risk of accidents.

Lack of sleep can also negatively affect your mental and emotional state. You may feel impatient or prone to mood swings. It can also damage the decision-making process and creativity. If sleep deprivation lasts long enough, you may begin to hallucinate—what you see or hear doesn't exist. Lack of sleep can also cause mania in people with bipolar disorder. Other psychological risks include:

- Impulsive behavior
- Anxiety
- Depression
- Paranoid
- Suicidal thoughts

You may also experience microsleep during the day. In these episodes, you will fall asleep for a few to a few seconds without realizing it. Lack of sleep is beyond your control, and it can be hazardous if you drive. If you operate heavy machinery at work and take naps, this may also make you more likely to get injured.

Immune System

When you sleep, your immune system produces protective anti-infective substances, such as antibodies and cytokines. It uses these substances to fight foreign invaders such as bacteria and viruses. Specific cytokines can also help you fall asleep and make your immune system more effective in defending against body diseases. Lack of sleep prevents your immune system from increasing its strength. If you don't get enough sleep, your body may not resist invaders, and it may take longer to recover. Long-term lack of sleep can also increase your risk of chronic diseases, such as diabetes and heart disease.

Respiratory System

The relationship between sleep and the respiratory system is two-way. Nocturnal breathing disorders called Obstructive Sleep Apnea can interrupt your sleep and reduce sleep quality. When you wake up all night, this can lead to a lack of sleep, making you more susceptible to respiratory infections such as the common cold and flu. Lack of sleep can also worsen existing respiratory diseases, such as chronic lung diseases.

Digestive System

In addition to eating too much and not exercising, lack of sleep is another risk factor for overweight and obesity. Sleep affects the levels of two hormones (leptin and ghrelin) to control hunger and fullness. Leptin tells the brain that you are full. Without enough sleep, your mind will reduce leptin and increase ghrelin, which is an appetite stimulant. These hormones' flux can explain why snacks are eaten at night or why someone overeats later in the evening.

Lack of sleep can also make you feel too tired to exercise. Over time, reducing exercise can lead to weight gain because you do not burn enough calories or increase muscle mass. Lack of sleep can also cause your body to release less insulin after eating. Insulin helps lower blood sugar (glucose) levels. Insufficient sleep can also reduce the body's tolerance to glucose and is related to insulin resistance. These damages can lead to diabetes and obesity.

Cardiovascular System

Sleep affects the processes that make your heart and blood vessels healthy, including those that affect blood sugar, blood pressure, and inflammation levels. It also plays a vital role in your body's ability to heal and repair blood vessels and heart. People with insufficient sleep are more likely to suffer from cardiovascular disease—an analysis linked insomnia to an increased risk of heart attack and stroke.

Endocrine System

The production of hormones depends on your sleep. To produce testosterone, you need at least 3 hours of uninterrupted sleep. Waking up all night may affect hormone production. This interruption can also affect the production of growth hormone, especially in children and adolescents. In addition to other growth functions, these hormones can also help the body build muscle mass and repair cells and tissues. The pituitary gland releases growth hormone every day, but adequate sleep and exercise also help release this hormone.

Lack of Sleep Can Cause Serious Health Problems

Heart Disease. Heart disease, such as coronary heart disease, heart attack, congestive heart failure, and congenital heart disease, is the leading cause of death for men and women in the United States. Preventive measures include quitting smoking, lowering cholesterol, controlling high blood pressure, maintaining a healthy weight, and exercising.

Heart Attack. A heart attack occurs when something prevents blood from flowing to your heart and cannot get the oxygen you need. More than one million Americans have a heart attack every year. A heart attack is also called a Myocardial Infarction (MI). It refers to muscle, "heart" refers to heart, and "infarction" refers to tissue death due to insufficient blood supply. This tissue death may cause permanent damage to your heart muscle.

Heart Failure. Heart failure can be caused by coronary artery disease, heart disease, cardiomyopathy, and high blood pressure. Heart failure treatment includes exercise prescribed by the doctor, dietary changes, medications, and minimal surgery.

Hypertension. High blood pressure or hypertension increases the risk of heart disease and stroke, and Risk factors for hypertension include obesity, excessive drinking, smoking, and family history. Beta-blockers are a standard treatment for hypertension.

Stroke. Strokes are caused by blocked blood vessels or bleeding in the brain. A stroke's signs include sudden severe headache, weakness, numbness, visual impairment, confusion, difficulty walking or speaking, dizziness, and slurred speech.

Diabetes. Diabetes is many diseases involving the hormone insulin. Naturally, the pancreas (the organ behind the stomach) releases insulin to help your body store and use the sugar and fat in your food. Diabetes occurs when the pancreas produces little or no insulin, or the body does not respond well to insulin. So far, there is no cure. People with diabetes need to control their disease to stay healthy.

Lack of Sleep Kills Libido

Sleep experts say that men and women who don't get enough sleep report that they have decreased libido and decreased interest in sex. Lack of energy, drowsiness, and increased tension may be the main reasons. For men with sleep apnea, a breathing problem that interrupts sleep may be another factor in decreased libido. A study showed that many men with sleep apnea also have low testosterone levels. In this study, nearly half of men with severe sleep apnea also secreted abnormally low testosterone levels at night.

Lack of Sleep Can Cause Skin Aging

After missing a few nights of sleep, most people have sagging skin and puffy eyes. But it turns out that long-term lack of sleep can lead to dull skin, fine lines, and dark circles. When you lack sleep, your body releases more stress hormone cortisol. Excessive cortisol will destroy skin collagen, a protein that keeps the skin smooth and elastic. Lack of sleep can also cause the body to release too little human growth hormone. When we are young, the human growth hormone can promote growth. As we age, it helps increase muscle mass, thicken the skin, and strengthen bones. "During deep sleep (which we call slow-wave sleep), growth hormone is released. This seems to be part of normal tissue repair-repairing the wear and tear of a day."

Sleepiness is Frustrating

Over time, lack of sleep and sleep disorders can lead to symptoms of depression. People diagnosed with depression or anxiety spends less than six hours asleep at night. Insomnia is the most common sleep disorder and has the most vital link with depression. In a 2007 study of 10,000 people, insomnia patients were five times more likely to suffer from depression than non-insomnia patients. Insomnia is usually one of the first symptoms of depression. Insomnia and depression affect each other. Lack of sleep usually exacerbates the symptoms of depression, and depression can make falling asleep more difficult. On the positive side, treating sleep problems can help depression and its symptoms, and vice versa.

The Main Causes Because I Can't Fall Asleep and Sleep Well

You may remember that you could fall asleep instantly and stay asleep happily after lunchtime the next day after some time. Now, your sleep is more likely to become more comfortable and healthier, and when you wake up in the morning, you may not always feel refreshed. Lack of quality sleep may be the natural result of changing sleep-wake patterns after menopause. The problem is also likely to be physical and solvable, and many conditions can disrupt your rest and be treated. It is essential to solve these problems. Lack of sleep not only makes you tired.

Chronic insomnia is associated with various health problems, including obesity, high blood pressure, heart disease, diabetes, and depression.

Sleep Apnea

The traditional image of sleep apnea is an overweight man who beats a man. Still, women of any size can also experience these repeated breathing pauses during sleep. "Women with narrow jaws or altered muscle tone will have apneas." Guidelines for health and longevity. These anatomical problems can prevent oxygen from reaching the lungs (and then the rest of the body) while you sleep. If you do have sleep apnea, beating may not be your main symptom, but you will find it unusually sleepy during the day.

Solution: Find an expert for sleep research. You can relieve apnea through some lifestyle adjustments, such as sleeping on your side or losing weight. Your doctor may also recommend oral appliances or CPAP machines to blow air into your airway to keep it open at night.

Diet

What you eat affects sleep. Spicy food can cause heartburn. Large meals can make you uncomfortable and increase obesity over time, which is a well-known risk factor for sleep apnea. Even if you end your coffee in the morning, too much caffeine can make you unable to sleep. "It takes six hours to remove half of the caffeine from the body. If you have enough caffeine, it will still be in your body at four in the morning." Although a glass of wine or two dinners together can make you feel relaxed and even sleepy, this will not help you fall asleep. "You can fall asleep, but once you fall asleep, you cannot fall asleep deeply."

Solution: Eat dinner at least a few hours before going to bed and keep your diet light. Avoid spicy, high-fat foods, as well as alcohol and caffeine. Also, do not drink too much liquid before going to bed. Having to get up often to go to the bathroom can also disrupt your sleep.

Lack of Exercise

Sleep and exercise are complementary. Regular exercise can help you sleep better. Conversely, if you sleep well, you are more likely to exercise.

Solution: Exercise every day as much as possible, preferably in the morning. Performing high-energy aerobic exercise too close to bedtime may have the opposite effect than expected, making you energetic and unable to fall asleep. However, a gentle yoga stretch before bed may not hurt. It can even help you relax.

Pain

Arthritis injury or any other kind of pain will not make you sleep well. On the contrary, lack of sleep can exacerbate your problem. Researchers believe that lack of sleep may activate inflammatory pathways and exacerbate arthritis pain. Lack of sleep can also make you more sensitive to pain.

Solution: In addition to the doctor's painkillers, try using a heating pad or take a hot bath before bed to relieve joint or muscle pain. Leaning on the body pillow can make you in a more comfortable posture while sleeping.

Restless Legs Syndrome

Women are twice as likely to suffer from Restless Legs Syndrome (RLS) as men. This condition can cause peristalsis at night, peristaltic sensations, and uncontrollable leg movements. It is usually related to hormonal changes in early life and during pregnancy, but RLS may continue as you age. RLS is not only very uncomfortable—researchers at Harvard University have linked this condition to women's increased risk of heart disease and depression.

Solution: Try a simple invasion first. Exercise every day, take a bath before bed, massage your legs, reduce caffeine and tobacco, and other things that may make you feel nervous. If these measures do not work, your doctor may recommend several medications to reduce RLS symptoms, like ropinirole and pramipexole.

Depression

"Depression is a simple compromiser of sleep, and it is much more common in women than in men." Depressed women may sleep more than usual, but their sleep isn't comfortable. Some of the antidepressants meant to check depression can also interfere with sleep.

Solution: See your initial care doctor, psychologist, psychiatrist, or therapist for help, including medications, talk therapy, etc. If your antidepressant seems to be holding you awake, ask your doctor to change you to another drug.

Stress

It isn't easy to sleep when the day's weight is pressing on you—finding a sense of calm before bed isn't comfortable—mostly when you can't unplug from the requirements of your day.

Solution: Determine the end time. Do a quiet, relaxing activity that does not involve the screen before going to bed. Chat with friends or family members, sew or read real books instead of using backlit tablet devices. "Just let yourself have a quiet time." Also, don't put your smartphone on the bedside table to sleep.

Poor Sleep Habits

Sometimes, insomnia is caused by long-term behavior, such as staying up late or doing stimulating activities before going to bed.

Solution: Follow some basic sleep hygiene strategies. Go to bed at the same time every day. Keep the bedroom cool, dark, and comfortable. Use your bed only for relaxation, sleep, and sex. If you cannot fall asleep within 15 minutes, please get up and leave the bedroom.

There are many possible reasons for insomnia, including your sleeping habits, lifestyle choices, and medical conditions. Some reasons are minor and can be improved through self-care, while others may require you to seek medical help. Causes of insomnia may include aging, excessive stimulation before going to bed (such as watching TV, playing video games or exercising), excessive caffeine intake, noise interference, uncomfortable bedroom, or feeling of excitement. Excessive sleep during the day, lack of sunlight, frequent urination, body aches, jet lag, and some prescription drugs may also cause sleep difficulties. For many people, stress, worry, frustration, or work schedule may also affect their sleep. For others, sleep problems are caused by sleep disorders, such as insomnia, sleep apnea, and restless legs syndrome.

Blu-Ray Insomnia

You hear the sound of turning off electronic devices about an hour before going to bedtime because the blue light emitted by these devices suppresses melatonin (a hormone that causes sleep). However, even the dazzling blue light emitted three or four hours ago (for example, watching TV during or shortly after dinner) is enough to delay melatonin production. However, you do not need to turn off the tube.

Menopause Insomnia

A drop in estrogen can cause discomfort in the middle of the night, including hot flashes. Studies have shown that about a quarter of menopausal women have sleep problems severe enough to affect their daytime functions. It is recommended to use moisture-wicking sheets and pajamas and then sleep on buckwheat pillows to prevent sweating. If your partner likes a warm bed, consider putting a separate bed cover on each bed's side.

Stealth Caffeine Insomnia

Intuitively, drinking coffee in the morning and afternoon will interfere with your future sleep. It is intuitive, but "people usually don't know that they are consuming other forms of caffeine, such as iced tea or chocolate." Everyone's metabolic charge is different, so you may be surprised when the caffeine should be cut off during the day. "If you cannot fall asleep, please eliminate it after lunch."

Freedom Insomnia

"Among older people, a positive aspect is that they often feel less stressed." However, this may mean that the schedule is out of date-making when you go to bed or wake up less critical. But these times will affect how your body releases melatonin later in the day. Even on weekends, keep as close as possible to the regular schedule.

Nap Insomnia

"Many adults do not take naps voluntarily or intentionally, but often fall asleep when they are not busy or watching TV." Either way, your brain sees it as sleep. The day's sleepiest time is between 2 and 3 in the afternoon when we experience a natural energy decline. It will prevent you from feeling tired at bedtime. So, spending too much time awake in bed can cause insomnia. If you don't have enough energy in the afternoon, please schedule activities for that time. It will support you feel refreshed, and research shows that the sleep quality of exercisers also has improved as a result, both earn money. Reading may be a manageable activity, but you should bring the book to the armchair instead of the bed. "I prefer the bed only for sleep and sex." Even calming activities such as puzzles or adult picture books may cause your brain to associate the bed with the activities you perform when you are awake. It may affect your ability to get up at night.

Insomnia Caused by Alcohol

Yes, a glass of wine can refresh you and make it easier to fall asleep. However, research shows that although it can help you soothe your emotions, it also has a rebounding effect and can make sleep more straightforward and more fragmented in the second half of the night. That's why you wake up at 3 in the morning, which also reduces the quality of sleep, so you don't have energy. Limit alcohol consumption three hours before going to bed and absorb it moderately.

Prescription for Insomnia

Low medication time can also disturb sleep. Some medicines, such as diuretics, can lower blood pressure and may make you have to urinate more frequently. More than one or two restrooms at night are abnormal. Other drugs, such as the antidepressant SSRI, may be stimulated or sedated depending on the type you use. Question your doctor about the best time to take the medications to ensure they do not interfere with your bedtime.

Anxiety Insomnia

Maybe you can fall asleep in one day, thanks to the "sleep pressure" during the day that prevents you from slipping asleep at night. But in the early hours of the morning, you may find yourself waking up and staring at the ceiling, full of worry. Your goal should not be to write down thoughts and things in the middle of the night to eliminate fears and solve the root cause. Cognitive-Behavioral Therapy for Insomnia (CBT-I) could help you rethink to reduce your brain's speed. A well-trained CBT-I therapist can help you, but there are also apps available to teach you these essential skills. "Don't just use them at 3 in the morning; use these apps for practice during the day. If you do want to use them at night, make assured to set your smartphone to the night setting so that the light does not make you more awake".

Insomnia Based on the Bedroom

Lay in bed, trying to force sleep to happen, in a boring backfire, it can persuade your brain that to be awake is normal. Instead, get up and go to another room and do something relaxing and calming under the dim light. It also helps to have an acceptance mentality. Sleep will come. If it's not tonight, don't sleep to make up for it—you might sleep better the next night. "Insomnia is also a symptom and a disease." If you improve your sleep habits (adhere to a regular sleep schedule, avoid drinking caffeine in the afternoon, etc.), but to no avail, your insomnia may be a symptom of another disease (such as depression or obstructive sleep apnea). If you have tried the above suggestions for a month but still cannot get enough sleep, please see a doctor for evaluation.

Chapter 2. How to Solve the Problems of Insomnia without Medicine?

What is Insomnia?

Many people think that the term "insomnia" refers to a complete lack of sleep. Insomnia includes many sleep problems, such as:

- Hard to fall asleep

- Wake up in the middle of the night

- Wake up early in the morning

- Restless sleep

Don't Be a Hero: The Harmful Effects of Insomnia

I heard someone brags that he or she only needs six hours of sleep? It is admirable to try to cope positively in adverse situations, but taking a bold attitude towards insomnia may be detrimental to your health. Most people need 7 to 9 hours of sleep. Lack of sleep can:

- Causes fatigue, irritability, and excessive daytime sleepiness

- Causes weight gain, making it difficult to lose weight

- Weaken the immune system and make you more likely to get sick

- Causes blood pressure to rise and may increase the risk of diabetes and heart disease

- Cause chronic pain

- Exacerbate mental illness, including depression and anxiety

- Reduce concentration and attention, leading to a decline in job performance

- Motor function declines, driving dangerous

- Technology to relieve insomnia without medication

Medications may be useful for certain things. Of course, certain natural or herbal sleep products may help you rest. But sleep prescription drugs are not always the best solution.

Unfortunately, some sleeping pills can make the problem worse. Sleep aids often interrupt the sleep cycle, resulting in less restorative sleep. Even if they help you fall asleep all night, your sleep is not necessarily profound or uncomfortable. People may rely on these drugs and ask them to fall asleep. Many people will develop tolerance to sleep medications repeatedly and require more drugs to achieve the same effect. These medications may also cause rebound insomnia, which means that it will be even more challenging to fall asleep without medication. Therefore, before taking this medicine for your sleep problems, try the following:

- Sleep hygiene
- Brief Cognitive Behavioral Therapy Interventions for Insomnia (also known as "CBT-I")

Sleep Hygiene

Sleep hygiene is several habits that can support you to fall asleep more quickly and sleep deeper. You can develop good sleep hygiene habits by yourself.

Sleep Hygiene: Matters Needing Attention

Things to do

- Stick to a regular sleep schedule (the same time to fall asleep and wake up time) seven days a week.

- Exercise at least 30 minutes a day for most of the week. Limit strenuous exercise to morning or afternoon. You can do more relaxing activities before going to bed, such as yoga poses that help you fall asleep.

- Get plenty of normal light during the day. Open the shades in the morning and go out during the day. You can even try to use the lightbox to help your brain wake up and regulate your body's rhythm in the dark winter morning.

- Establish a regular relaxing bedtime program.

- Take a hot bath or shower before going to bed.

- Perform relaxation exercises before going to bed, including paying attention to breathing and progressive muscle relaxation.

- Make sure your sleeping atmosphere is comfortable and pleasant. Your bed should be relaxed, and the room should not be too hot, too cold, or too bright. If necessary, use earplugs and eye masks. Make sure your pillow is comfortable.

- Only connect the bed with sleep and sex. Do not work, eat or watch TV in bed.

- Go to bed when you are drowsy and get up if you toss and turn.

- Turn the clock so that you can't see the time.

- Turn off SMS and email alerts on your phone.

- Keep a "worry diary." If you have any thoughts while trying to fall asleep, please write them down to revisit the next day.

- If you still cannot fall asleep after about 20 minutes, please leave the bed and relax (for example, reading); go to bed later.

- Download free screen dimming software for your computer. Flux and Dimmer are two popular programs. If you utilize your computer late at night, these beautiful programs can avoid irritating bright light. Even better: put your laptop away an hour before going to bed!

Don't

- Do not consume caffeine in the afternoon. These include coffee, tea, iced tea, energy drinks, and soda water.

- Don't drink the second glass of wine at dinner. As we all know, drinking alcohol will speed up sleep. Still, it can also disrupt sleep; notably, in the second half of the night, when the human body should enter deep sleep, it will cause arousal.

- Do not take other stimulants, including chocolate, nicotine, and certain drugs, before going to bed.

- Don't eat a high meal before going to bed.

- Don't watch TV, use a computer, or spend long hours on mobile devices before bed. These exercises stimulate the brain and make it more difficult to fall.

- Do not use cell phones, laptops, or other mobile devices in bed.

- Don't succumb to the desire to take a nap during the day; it interferes with standard sleep/wake patterns.

Insomnia is more than the occasional difficulty of falling asleep or staying asleep. Most people experience sleep disorders at some point in their lives. If you have a chronic disease (meaning that you have more nights and nights,) and it is difficult to fall asleep or staying asleep. You will not feel refreshed in the morning, especially if they lack sleep starts to affect your personal or professional life, and it may be time to seek medical help.

There are many possible causes of insomnia, including sleep apnea, restless legs syndrome, thyroid problems, or other underlying medical conditions. However, most people who struggle with sleep do not have inherent medical issues. For them, sleep hygiene alone usually restores their ability to get a good, peaceful sleep every night. However, if good sleep hygiene is not enough to solve your insomnia, please cooperate with therapist training in Cognitive Behavioral Therapy for Insomnia (CBT-I).

What Is Cognitive-Behavioral Therapy for Insomnia?

CBT-I is a solution to the behavior that prevents you from falling asleep virtually, and the thought that may interfere with sleep. The behavioral aspects of CBT-1 focus on stimulus control and sleep restriction.

How Does Stimulus Control Work?

CBT-I goes beyond basic sleep hygiene principles (such as reducing caffeine intake and creating a "relaxation" period before bedtime) to study stimulus control deeper. The goal is to enhance the bed as a cue to sleep and weaken the bed to wake up. These are the basic principles of stimulus control:

Establish A Regular Wake-Up Time. Although you may be told that establishing a regular bedtime is the key to avoid insomnia, setting a standard wake-up time is more effective. Keep up the time even on weekends. It will help you get enough morning light and help regulate the body's natural sleep/wake cycle.

Go to Bed Only When You Are Sleepy. It is essential to distinguish fatigue from sleepiness. Fatigue is a low phase of physical and mental energy, but this in itself is not the reason for trying to sleep. Drowsiness is an effort to stay awake, such as doping while watching TV or riding a train. Eventually, establish a regular bedtime. After a good night's sleep, you will have a good understanding of your "natural" bedtime. Unless you are not sleepy, please stick to bedtime.

Don't Lie Awake in Bed. If you cannot fall asleep, or wake up in the middle of the night but cannot return to sleep immediately, get up, and do some quiet and relaxing things, such as reading. Only go back to bed when you want to sleep again.

Avoid Naps During the Day. For people who do not have insomnia, rest is not necessarily a bad thing. But for those with insomnia problems, naps can further disrupt the body's sleep/wake cycle. As far as CBT-I is concerned, do not sleep during the day.

The Core of CBT-I: Sleep Restriction

Sleep restriction to treat insomnia seems counterintuitive. However, this therapy is beneficial in restoring insomnia (so to speak). Studies have shown that 75% to 80% of people see significant improvement within four weeks of starting sleep restriction with a CBT-1 therapist. Since it is difficult to properly maintain a sleep restriction schedule when solving problems that cause insomnia, it is important to only practice sleep restriction with a trained CBT-I therapist or healthcare provider who can help you deal with potential challenges. Sleep restriction works as follows:

- Your therapist will ask you to calculate the average amount of sleep per night. In the bedside diary, record how much time you sleep each night. After a week, calculate your average sleep time per night. That is your starting point.

- Assume that your average sleep time per night in the first week is 6 hours. Next week, if your alarm is set to 8:00 AM, please go to bed 6 hours before that time. In this example, you will go to bed at 2:00 AM. After a few days, you should notice a decrease in your sense of wakefulness at midnight. If you are unwilling, please consult your therapist.

- After restricting sleep for a week, your therapist will suggest increasing your sleep time by 30 minutes (assuming that your nighttime wakefulness is kept to a minimum). In this example, you will now go to bed at 1:30 AM.

- After going to bed at 1:30 in the morning for a week, add another 30 minutes of sleep time. Continue to increase your sleep time by 30 minutes each week until you get about 8 hours of restful sleep every night.

- If you start to be visibly awake in the middle of the night, your therapist may recommend restoring more sleep restrictions to return to normal.

If you feel tired during the first few weeks of sleep restriction, don't lose heart. It is widespread. As you reset your body's sleep clock, you will gradually begin to experience more peaceful sleep.

Don't Forget the Initials of Good Sleep Hygiene

If you have established good sleep hygiene habits, CBT-I works best. It is essential to reduce arousal and activation and avoid the intake of certain substances. Here is a brief review:

- Keep the bedtime habit, which involves an hour of relaxation time to relax and cause drowsiness.

- Avoid exercising within four hours before going to bed.

- Avoid exposure to intense light (especially TV or computer screens) during the one-hour sleep period.

- Create a comfortable, pleasant, and quiet sleeping environment in your bedroom.

- Avoid looking at the clock; otherwise, it will cause anxiety.

- Transform cognition from "working hard to fall asleep" to "allowing sleep to happen."

- Avoid caffeinated foods and drinks afternoon.

- Avoid taking caffeine-containing drugs at bedtime.

- Don't eat a meal before bed, and don't eat snacks late at night.

- Relax alcohol. Alcohol can make falling asleep more comfortable, but it can increase toss and turns in the second half of the night.

- Do not smoke. Smoking and nicotine withdrawal (quitting smoking) both interfere with sleep. The best choice is to quit smoking before starting CBT-I.

Unhelpful Thinking Can Stop Sleep

Where does the treatment fit the equation? In addition to behavior, your thoughts about sleep often prevent you from getting enough sleep. A therapist trained in CBT-I can help you discover harmful ideas and teach you how to challenge and change your thoughts. For persistent sleep worries, your therapist may recommend a "worry diary" to write down all the things that bother you or set a specified time for concerns. The goal of both strategies is to consider all these issues before going to bed. If nightmares or anxiety disturb your sleep, there may be a more suitable treatment for you.

Best Remedies

Many people feel short-term insomnia. This general sleep disorder can make it difficult to fall asleep and staying asleep. Although the quantity of sleep needed varies from person to person, most adults require at least seven hours of sleep each night. If your sleeping style is affecting your quality of life, home remedies may help. Read on to learn how to control your sleep style through meditation, exercise, and other home remedies.

Mindfulness Meditation

Mindfulness meditation involves slow and steady breathing while sitting still. You will observe the rise and disappearance of breath, body, thoughts, feelings, and sensations. Mindfulness meditation has many health benefits, and they are inseparable from a healthy lifestyle that promotes good sleep. It is said to reduce stress, improve concentration, and enhance immunity. In a 2011 study, researchers found that meditation significantly improved insomnia and overall sleep patterns. Participants took part in a weekly meditation class, a one-day retreat, and practiced at home for several months.

You can meditate as you like. If you don't have time to exercise for a more extended period, please exercise for 15 minutes in the morning or evening. Consider participating in a meditation group once a week to stay motivated. You can also choose to conduct an online guided meditation. Meditation is safe to practice, but it can cause strong emotions. If you think this will cause further anxiety or turbulence, please stop practicing.

The Mantra Is Repeated

Saying the mantra repeatedly and surely will help you focus and calm your mind. Mantras create a feeling of relaxation by calming the mind. Researchers taught homeless women to repeat the spell silently during the day, and before going to bed in a 2015 study, using the mantra for a week had reduced insomnia. You can choose the mantra of Sanskrit, English, or other languages. Search for ideas online or create ideas that suit you. Choose a spell that makes you feel happy and calm. In the present tense, this should be a simple, positive statement. A good mantra will keep you focused on the repetition of the sound to relax and fall asleep.

Recite the mantra quietly or loudly, focusing on the words. Whenever it lingers, gently bring your mind back to the spell. You can also play music by chanting. Recite your mantra anytime, anywhere. You can choose another attack to use during the day. If you feel that chanting causes any discomfort or irritability, please stop practicing.

Yoga

Yoga has been discovered to have a positive impact on sleep quality. Yoga can also reduce stress, improve physical function, and enhance mental concentration. Choose a style that concentrates more on meditation or breathing activities rather than challenging physical exercises. Slow and controlled movements can keep you immersed and focused. Yin and restorative yoga are good choices. Strive to do it a few times a week and practice at least 20 minutes a day. Posing before bed can help you relax and relax. If the posture is not suitable for you, please do not force it. Forcible use may cause injury. Doing jobs that are good for you and your body is essential, and it varies from person to person.

Exercise

Exercise can improve overall health. It can enhance mood, make you energetic, help lose weight, and improve sleep. Participants in the 2015 study exercised at least 150 minutes a week from a trusted source for six months. During this time, the researchers found that the participants' insomnia symptoms were significantly reduced. They also showed a reduction in symptoms of depression and anxiety.

To get these benefits, you should do at least 20 minutes of moderate exercise every day. You may increase strength training or aerobic exercise several times a week. Find the time that best suits your needs and has the most positive impact on your sleep. Consider your physical condition and exercise accordingly. It may cause personal injury, but if you exercise caution, you can usually avoid damage.

Massage

In a 2015 study, researchers found that massage therapy can benefit patients with insomnia by improving sleep quality and daytime dysfunction. It can also relieve feelings of pain, anxiety, and depression. If you cannot choose a professional massage, you can perform a self-massage. You may also find it beneficial for your partner or friend to massage you. As your mind roams, let your mind focus on the sensation and feeling of touch—online research tips and tricks. Generally speaking, massage is safe, but if you have any specific health problems that may hinder its benefits, please consult a doctor. If your skin is receptive to creams or oils, perform a skin patch test before use.

Magnesium

Magnesium is a natural mineral. It can support muscles to relax and relieve stress. It is believed that this can promote a healthy way of sleeping. Participants in the 2012 study took 500 milligrams (mg) of magnesium daily for two months. During this time, the researchers discovered that participants had fewer symptoms of insomnia and improved sleep patterns. Men may take 400 mg per day, and women may take 300 mg per day. You can choose to divide the dose between morning and evening or take it before going to bed.

You can also combine 1 cup of magnesium tablets to the bath in the evening to allow magnesium to be received through the skin. Side effects include stomach and intestinal problems. You may want to start with a lower dose and gradually increase the amount to see how your body responds. Taking it with food may reduce abdominal discomfort. If you take any medications, consult your doctor to determine potential interactions. You should not take magnesium supplements regularly. Take a few days off every two weeks. Do not take more than the dosage recommended on the product.

Lavender Oil

Lavender is used to improving mood, relieve pain, and promote sleep. It is considered more efficient when taken orally. The results of a 2014 study showed that when taken with antidepressants, lavender essential oil capsules help improve the sleep patterns of depression patients. People also offer lower levels of anxiety, which seems to improve sleep. Take 20 to 80 mg of lavender by mouth every day, or as directed. You may wish to add lavender essential oil to the diffuser or spray it on the pillow. Lavender tea is also an option. Lavender is usually safe to use. Taking lavender by mouth may cause headaches, constipation, or nausea.

Melatonin

Melatonin can help you fall asleep faster and improve sleep quality. In a 2016 study, researchers found that melatonin can significantly improve cancer and insomnia patients' sleep patterns. Between 7 and 14 days, sleep quality has been further enhanced. Take 1 to 5 mg 30 minutes to two hours before going to bed. It would be best if you used the lowest effective dose possible because higher doses may cause side effects, such as:

- Depression
- Dizziness
- Headache
- Irritability
- Stomach cramps
- Sober night

Melatonin is usually safe to use in a short time.

Chapter 3. Foods for Better Sleep

If you have been counting calories and going to the gym, but staying up all night to complete the Netflix marathon, you may hinder your progress. For your body to serve at its optimal level, you need to balance exercise, diet, and sleep time. Exercise, diet, and sleep together form the basis of long-term health and well-being. Working a healthy diet can help you fall asleep quickly, improve the quality and duration of sleep, and get a stable and high-quality sleep can help you eat better. Studies have shown that you are more likely to consume foods high in calories, fats, and sugars when you are sleep deprived. That will discuss the best sleep-promoting diet, what it looks like, things to avoid before going to bed, and how to use diet to get adequate sleep.

What Should Your Sleep Diet Look Like?

Your sleep diet is much like the diet you have been trying to lose weight. Sleep-promoting diets are varied, rich in fruits, vegetables, whole grains, lean protein, and dairy products. Be wary of sleep supplements; the effect is not as described in the advertisement. A healthy sleep diet can also control portion size and limit the amount of high-sugar and heavily processed foods you consume daily. The nutrients found in a range of healthy foods are particularly beneficial for sleep.

Is There Any Food to Keep You Awake?

Although many foods are good for sleep, other foods may cause sleep difficulties. Foods that interfere with sleep include high-sugar, high-carbohydrate, and heavily processed foods. The same junk food can also cause trouble for your waistline and risk for your sleep. Eating sugary foods during the day can cause significant blood sugar changes, causing fatigue, which can change your daily work and sleep patterns at night. A meal high in carbohydrates has a similar effect on blood sugar. Eating a full meal close to bedtime will interfere with the body's process of relaxing sleep.

Should I Eat and Drink Before Going to Bed?

In other words, sleeping hungry is not a good idea. An empty and rumbling belly can be distracting and make falling asleep more difficult. Nevertheless, it is best to avoid eating at bedtime. Too full bedtime may also affect falling asleep, and due to the body's digestion, the quality of sleep throughout the night may be disturbed. If you must eat before going to bed, and then choose some snacks, such as yogurt, bananas, a small bowl of low-sugar cereals, or even night smoothies to lose weight are a wise choice.

You want to drink as much water as possible. Staying hydrated throughout the day promotes alertness and concentration, and helps minimize changes in energy levels. Dehydration can lead to feeling tired and tired, and may eventually disrupt sleep patterns. By the time you feel thirsty, you are already dehydrated. Drinking water during the day can help you maintain energy levels and avoid dehydration to prepare for the rest of the night. Avoid drinking adult beverages in the late afternoon, because alcohol can cause snoring and aggravate sleep apnea. Other drinks such as tea and juice can also help you stay hydrated. Still, it is best to limit sugary drinks or avoid sugary drinks altogether. Eating sugary or caffeinated beverages can enhance mental clarity and alertness, which is very important for many people, especially in the morning.

Better sleep is essential to your overall health. It can reduce your risk of certain chronic diseases, keep your brain healthy, and strengthen your immune system. It is usually recommended that you keep 7-9 hours of uninterrupted sleep every night. However, many people struggle to get enough sleep. You can use various strategies to promote good sleep, including changing your eating habits, because certain foods and beverages have sleep-promoting properties.

Almonds

Almond is a nut with multiple health benefits. They are an outstanding source of several nutrients because 1 ounce (28 grams) of dry roasted nuts contains 18% of the daily phosphorus and 23% of riboflavin for adults. An ounce also meets 25% of men's daily manganese requirements and 31% of women's daily manganese requirements. Regular consumption of almonds is associated with a lower risk of some chronic diseases, such as type 2 diabetes and heart disease. It is due to their healthy monounsaturated fats, fiber, and antioxidants.

Antioxidants can protect your cells from harmful inflammation that can cause these chronic diseases. It is said that almonds can also help improve sleep quality. It is because almonds and several other nuts are sources of melatonin. Melatonin controls your internal clock and signals your body to prepare for sleep. Almonds are also an excellent magnesium source, and only 1 ounce can meet 19% of your daily needs. A sufficient intake of magnesium may help improve sleep quality, especially for those who have insomnia.

The use of magnesium in improving sleep is believed to be related to its ability to reduce inflammation. It may also help reduce the stress hormone cortisol level, which is known to disrupt sleep. However, despite this, there are still few studies on almonds and sleep. A study examined the effects of feeding 400 milligrams (mg) of the almond extract on rats. The study found that compared with not eating almond extract, rats sleep longer and more in-depth. The potential sleep-related impacts of almonds are promising, but more inclusive human studies are needed. If you desire to eat almonds before going to bed to determine whether they affect your sleep quality, a 1 ounce (28 g) serving or about a small number of almonds is sufficient.

Turkey

Turkey is delicious and nutritious. The protein content is high; roast turkey can provide nearly 8 grams of protein per ounce (28 grams). Protein is essential for keeping muscles healthy and regulating appetite. Turkey is also a moderate source of small amounts of vitamins and minerals, such as riboflavin and phosphorus. It is an excellent selenium source, with 3 ounces per ounce, providing 56% of the Daily Value (DV).

Turkey has some characteristics that explain why some people feel tired after eating, or think that this encourages lethargy. Most notably, it carries the amino acid tryptophan, which can increase the production of melatonin. The protein in turkey may also help promote fatigue. There is evidence that eating a moderate amount of protein before bed can improve sleep quality, including reducing the time to wake up all night.

Chamomile Tea

Chamomile tea is a modern herbal tea that provides multiple health benefits. It is famous for its flavonoids. Flavonoids are antioxidants that reduce inflammation, managing chronic diseases such as cancer and heart disease. There is also proof that drinking chamomile tea can strengthen your immune system, reduce anxiety and depression, and improve skin health. Also, chamomile tea has some unique characteristics that can enhance the quality of sleep.

Specifically, chamomile tea contains apigenin. This antioxidant binds to specific receptors in the brain to promote sleepiness and reduce insomnia. A 2011 study conducted on 34 adults and found that compared with people who did not consume the extract, those who took 270 mg of chamomile extract a day for 28 days had a 15-minute increase in falling asleep; the time to wake up was reduced by 15 minutes. Another research found that women who drank chamomile tea for two weeks had improved sleep quality compared to women who did not drink tea. Those who drink chamomile tea also have fewer depression symptoms, which is usually related to sleep problems. If you want to develop sleep quality, drinking chamomile tea before bed is undoubtedly worth trying.

Kiwi

Kiwi is a low-calorie and nutritious fruit. A kind of fruit contains only 42 calories and many nutrients, including 71% vitamin C DV. It gives men and women 23% and 31% of the daily vitamin K required. It contains moderate amounts of folic acid and potassium and several trace minerals. Also, eating kiwi fruit may benefit your digestive health, reduce inflammation, and lower cholesterol. These effects are because they provide a lot of fiber and carotenoid antioxidants.

According to research on the potential to improve sleep quality, kiwi fruit may also be one of the healthiest foods to eat before bed. In a 4-week study, 24 adults ate two kiwis one hour before going to bed every night. At the end of the course, the participants' falling asleep speed increased by 42% compared with not eating before going to bed. Their ability to sleep without waking up all night increased by 5%, while their total sleep time increased by 13%.

The sleep-promoting effect of kiwi is sometimes attributed to serotonin. Serotonin is a brain chemical that supports to improve your sleep cycle. It has also been suggested that the anti-inflammatory antioxidants in kiwi, such as vitamin C and carotenoids, may be partly due to its sleep-promoting effects. More scientific proof is needed to determine the effect of kiwifruit on improving sleep. However, eating 1-2 moderate kiwis before bed may help you fall asleep faster and stay asleep longer.

Tart Cherry Juice

Tart cherry juice has some remarkable health benefits. First, it provides the right amount of essential nutrients, such as magnesium and phosphorus. It is also a good source of potassium. In 8 ounces (240 milliliters) of food, women need 17% of potassium per day, and men need 13% of potassium per day. Also, it is a rich origin of antioxidants, including anthocyanins and flavanols. Tart cherry juice can also promote sleepiness and has even been studied for reducing insomnia. For these purposes, taking tart cherry juice before bed may develop your sleep quality. The sleep-promoting effect of tart cherry juice is due to its large amount of melatonin.

In a study, adults with insomnia drank 8 ounces (240 ml) of tart cherry juice twice a day for two weeks. Compared with the time without juice, they slept for 84 minutes and reported better sleep quality. Although these results are encouraging, more extensive research is needed to confirm tart cherry juice's role in improving sleep and preventing insomnia. However, if you have difficulty falling asleep or falling asleep at night, it is worth trying some tart cherry juice before bed.

Fatty Fish

Fatty fish like salmon, tuna, trout, and mackerel are very healthy. What makes them unique is their vitamin D content. For example, a 3 ounce (85 g) serving of salmon contains 570 international units (IU) of vitamin D. This is 71% of your DV. Similar farmed rainbow trout servings account for 81% of your DV. Also, fatty fish is rich in healthy omega-3 fatty acids, such as Eicosatetraenoic Acid (EPA) and Docosahexaenoic Acid (DHA).

EPA and DPA can reduce inflammation. Also, omega-3 fatty acids can prevent heart disease and promote brain health.

The mixture of omega-3 fatty acids and vitamin D in obese fish can enhance sleep quality because both have been shown to increase serotonin production. In one study, people who ate 10.5 ounces (300 grams) of Atlantic salmon three times a week fell asleep 10 minutes faster than people who ate chicken, beef, or pork for six months. This effect is considered the result of vitamin D. The vitamin D content in fish schools is higher, which is related to the significant development in sleep quality. Eating several ounces of fatty fish before bed may help you fall asleep faster and sleep deeper. For fatty fish's ability to improve sleep, more research is needed to draw a clear conclusion.

Walnut

Walnut is a popular nut. They are rich in nutrients, in addition to providing 1.9 grams of fiber per 1 ounce (28 grams), they also offer more than 19 types of vitamins and minerals. Walnuts are incredibly rich in magnesium, phosphorus, manganese, and copper. Furthermore, walnuts are an essential source of healthy lipids, including omega-3 fatty acids and linoleic acid. They also give 4.3 grams of protein per ounce, which may help reduce appetite. Walnuts can also enhance heart health. Their ability to reduce high cholesterol levels has been studied, and cholesterol is a significant risk factor for heart disease.

Some researchers also claim that eating walnuts can improve sleep quality because they are among the best food sources of melatonin. The fatty acid content of walnuts may also help improve sleep. They give Alpha-Linolenic Acid (ALA), an omega-3 fatty acid converted into DHA in the body. DHA may increase the production of serotonin. There is not much evidence to support the claim that walnuts improve sleep. There has not been any research on their role in promoting sleep. In any case, if you are not getting enough sleep, eating some walnuts before bed may help. About a few walnuts are a good part.

Passion Fruit Tea

Passion fruit tea is another herbal tea traditionally used to treat a variety of health diseases. It is a rich origin of flavonoid antioxidants. Flavonoid antioxidants are known for reducing inflammation, enhancing immune health, and reducing heart disease risk. Also, passion fruit tea has been studied for its potential to reduce anxiety. The antioxidant apigenin may be the reason that passionflower reduces stress. Apigenin creates a calming effect by binding to specific receptors in the brain. There is also evidence that passionflower increases the production of the brain chemical Gamma-Aminobutyric Acid (GABA). The role of GABA is to inhibit other brain chemicals that can cause stress, such as glutamate.

The calming properties of passion fruit tea may promote drowsiness, so drinking tea before bed may be beneficial. In the 7-day study, 41 adults drank a cup of passion fruit tea before going to bed. Their evaluation of sleep quality with tea is much better than without tea.

White Rice

It is a grain that is widely used as a staple food in many countries. The main difference between white rice and brown rice is that the bran and germ of white rice have been removed. It reduces its fiber, nutrients, and antioxidant content. Despite this, white rice still contains a considerable number of vitamins and minerals. 4 ounces (79 grams) of white rice can meet 19% of your daily folate needs. It also provides 21% of men's daily thiamine requirements and 22% of women's daily thiamine requirements. The DV content of manganese in 4 ounces (79 grams) of long-grain white rice flour is 13%.

White rice is high in carbohydrates, providing 22 grams per 4 ounces (79 grams). Its carbohydrate content and lack of fiber provide its high glycemic index (GI). The glycemic index is a measure of how fast-food increases blood sugar. Some people suggest that eating high-GI foods, such as white rice, at least 1 hour before bedtime, may improve sleep quality. A study compared the sleep habits of 1,848 people based on their rice, bread, or noodle intake. Compared with bread or noodles, high rice intake is associated with better sleep, including longer sleep time. Although eating white rice may have a sleep-promoting effect, it is best eaten in moderation due to its relatively low fiber and nutrients.

Day Diet for a Night's Sleeping Well

The first step in improving sleep is to eat balanced, nutritious meals and snacks evenly throughout the day. Eat too little during the day, and at night you will overeat, leading to tossing and turning and indigestion throughout the day. If you eat too small for dinner, you may find yourself lying awake in bed, eager to go to the refrigerator.

If you have gastrointestinal problems, such as gluten or lactose intolerance, eating certain foods at night can also disrupt your sleep. Take some time to learn about your gastrointestinal triggers, such as spicy foods or alcohol, and avoid using them so you can get rid of the discomfort. It is also essential to fall asleep and wake up at the same time every day-experts say this will keep your stomach and brain sleeping at similar times.

Skip Sugar and Caffeine

Using more than three 8-ounce cups of caffeine per day may affect sleep, and six or more coffee cups are considered too much. Since the human body needs about 6 hours to metabolize caffeine, it is not recommended to drink or consume caffeine-containing food within a few hours after turning off the lights. It is essential to remember that people respond differently to caffeine, so find a way of consumption that suits you.

Sugar is also related to sleep problems. One study found that children with type 1 diabetes have more difficulty falling asleep if blood sugar rises. Because sugar can temporarily increase energy, it is best to avoid sugar and other processed foods before bed.

Reaching Complex Carbohydrates

Studies have shown that the best bedtime snacks contain a variety of carbohydrates and a small amount of protein, such as cereals with milk or a small piece of whole wheat bread with a little peanut butter. Research shows that eating most of the recommended daily amount of carbohydrates at night can help if you want to fall asleep quickly. Researchers found that when participants ate a carbohydrate-rich dinner that included high-glycemic-index jasmine rice instead of low-GI long-grain rice, they fell asleep faster. Researchers speculate that insulin triggered by a high-GI diet can cause more sleep-inducing tryptophan in the brain more quickly.

Drink a Soothing Drink

Although the research results of chamomile tea are mixed, some people still swear. A clinical trial found that chamomile can reduce anxiety in humans, and large doses can help animals fall asleep. Still, more experiments are needed to understand whether chamomile is equally applicable to humans. A 2011 study published a hot drink, which can help people reduce their feelings of loneliness and increase their security sense. Both of these factors can promote a good night's sleep.

If you have a confusing stomach late at night, then the old lady's legend that peppermint tea is helpful may be right. They found that peppermint tea is a digestive aid and may even have anti-allergic potential-meaning. It can help you sleep more peacefully.

Boost Your B Vitamins

The belief that turkey makes you tired may be a bit exaggerated due to its high tryptophan levels, which produces serotonin. Tryptophan and bird's B vitamins can still improve night sleep. Still, they won't immediately bring the feeling you think after a Thanksgiving dinner. It turns out that vitamin B6, found in foods such as poultry, fish, chickpeas, and bananas, helps your body process tryptophan and convert it into sleep-inducing serotonin more quickly. You can get the suggested daily amount of 1 to 1.5 mg of B6 by eating two to three servings of B6-rich food every day.

Make Room for Milk

The "a cup of warm milk" adage is so famous for a reason: certain nutrients in milk, such as tryptophan and B vitamins, can be used as natural sleep aids. To maintain normal sleep and three to four servings of low-fat or skimmed dairy products are consumed every day. Consider energy drinks, even unexpected sources, such as decaffeinated coffee and tea. A famous coffee shop study showed that some decaffeinated coffee contained more than 13 mg of caffeine in a 16-ounce serving, which is as much as some caffeinated beverages in the coffee shop. Other surprising caffeine sources can include certain non-cola sodas, chocolate and cocoa products, ice cream, and breakfast cereals. Of course, these are not the only sneaky dietary sources of sleep-damaging chemicals. Here are some other foods and drinks to limit or avoid before going to bed to better sleep.

Alcohol

Studies have shown that fit people who drink alcohol do fall asleep faster and sleep deeper...at first. However, after alcohol disappears, it wakes people up during a significant restorative sleep phase. Alcohol can also exacerbate sleep apnea symptoms, and if used regularly, it can also increase your chances of sleepwalking, lack of sleep, and memory loss.

For Better Sleep: drink a glass of sour cherry juice before going to bed. Tart cherries are a real cause of the hypnotic hormone melatonin.

Spicy Food

Eating spicy food can cause heartburn, affecting your sleep. When you lie down, acid reflux usually gets worse. If you have sleep apnea, your signs may worsen if the backup acid irritates your airways.

Moreover, studies have shown that eating red pepper will increase your core body temperature, which is destructive because it will naturally drop during sleep. (Overheating makes it more difficult for the body to perform this temperature conversion.)

For Better Sleep: Avoid spicy foods within three hours before going to bed. If ketchup and other acidic foods can cause heartburn or indigestion, you should do the same.

High-Fat and High-Protein Food

In one study, rats on a high-fat diet for eight consecutive weeks had more dispersed sleep at night and excessive sleepiness during the day. It may be because high-fat foods increase weight and reduce sensitivity to the brain chemical orexin, thereby regulating the body's sleep clock. High-protein foods (such as steak and chicken) can also disrupt sleep because they take a long time to break down, which is a problem at bedtime. After all, the digestion rate is reduced by 50% during sleep. If you eat a great meal before bed, your body will face a similar challenge. Also, avoid aged or processed cheeses, salami, and pepperoni: they contain tyramine, will trigger the release of norepinephrine, thereby stimulating the brain.

For Better Sleep: Eat complex carbohydrates before going to bed, such as whole-wheat toast or oatmeal bowl. These foods trigger the release of the sleep serotonin, and the digestion time is not long.

Foods to Avoid Before Going to Bed

We lose sleep on too many things, so the last thing we need to do is make late-night dining decisions that are not good for us. Everyone likes to nap at night, but your decision to eat something will significantly affect your sleep quality. Although some foods can help you sleep, other foods (fatty or greasy foods) can wreak havoc on your rest.

Ice Cream

A bowl of ice cream may be the most comfortable accompaniment to a bad breakup bed, but its soothing properties are limited. For starters, ice cream is rich in fat, so you won't give your body a chance to burn it before going to bed, and then all the sugar will fill your body with energy before you hit the ice cream, so you will send different messages physically. Most importantly, sugar has just been stored and turned into fat, so this is a lose-lose situation. It has also been found that eating high-sugar foods before going to bed can cause nightmares, so although the taste may be calm, the results are disturbing.

Celery

You may be surprised to see celery on this list. Still, there is a simple reason: celery is a natural diuretic. It means it will make you pee more than usual. Diuretics increase the speed of urination by pushing water into the system. Therefore, this means that if you soak too much celery before going to bed, your body may wake you up from sleep and make you pee. Vegetables are the most nutritious food you can provide to your body. Still, please avoid eating celery and other foods to prevent poor sleep.

Pasta

For those who desire a quick bite before going to bed, pasta is a quick and easy solution, but it is not your ideal night snack. Pasta is pure carbohydrates; if you go to bed after eating, everything will become fat. Most importantly, the things added to the pasta—oil, cheese, and thick cream or tomato sauce—will only increase your caring crowd. Also, most pasta has a substantial glycemic index, which means it is more likely to work with blood sugar levels to delay sleep and wake you up at night.

Pizza

If you want to do abdominal exercises before going to bed, you can add some greasy, salty pizza to it. When most other organs are also cold, your stomach will want to relax like the rest of your body, but pizza is not a light meal. Your stomach must be busy. The ketchup layer has a high acidity, which is just another catalyst for acid reflux. Still, in general, fatty and greasy ingredients (especially high-fat meats and cheeses) can play an excellent role when stirred Heartburn. That's not the wake-up call you want at night. If you're going to do this, treat your stomach well, and check these nutritious pizza fillings.

Candy Bar

If the nightmare about the monster in the closet or the little monster under the bed disturbs your sleep, you may want to avoid eating sweets. One of the easiest (and worst) ways to get out of deep sleep is what we dream of real. A recent study showed that seven out of ten people are more likely to eat junk food, such as candy, before going to bed. The hypothesis is that high sugar content will produce more nightmarish brain waves.

Try to use these junk food alternatives. If you want to spend a calm night, please remove this late-night snack from the list.

Cereals

Mitt Romney likes to drink a bowl of cold cereal before going to bed, but he may want to be careful about the one he chooses. Otherwise, he won't get the other food he needs. Cereals usually contain a lot of refined sugar and are rich in carbohydrates. It may cause your blood sugar levels to rise suddenly and collapse, which is not ideal for calming your body before going to bed. Instead of pursuing sugary grains, it is better to seek healthier grains. Those whole-grain foods with low sugar content can eliminate food cravings, but will not keep you healthy.

Garlic

If you sleep in the same bed with your partner, you may wish to avoid garlic before going to bed, but apart from bad breath, it is best to avoid garlic. Garlic is called a "hot herb" and, along with spicy foods, tends to have specific properties that cause heartburn. As we all know, sometimes, this practice has the side effect of making the stomach upset, so if your stomach is weak or prone to acid reflux, the last thing you need to do is to start the fire before lying down and resting.

Dark Chocolate

Who doesn't like to sneak a bit of chocolate before going to bed to get that warm feeling? Unfortunately, if you desire a good night's sleep, dark chocolate is one of the best foods you avoid. Dark chocolate is a sneaky cause of caffeine and is known to cheer you up. Almost all chocolates hold a certain amount of caffeine. The most important thing is that chocolate also contains stimulants such as theobromine, making your heartbeat. The cheapest way is white chocolate, which does not contain theobromine and usually lacks caffeine.

Wine

It is generally believed that a lot of alcohol will make you addicted and produce good sleep, but this is not entirely accurate. Although drinking can help you fall asleep, it will not bring you a lasting and refreshing rest. Alcohol interferes with the vital function of sleep, usually paving the way for light rest and several waking hours throughout the night. Most importantly, people who frequently drink and fall asleep will become more and more dependent on alcohol, leading to a frustrating cycle. If you want a deep, peaceful sleep, you should avoid drinking alcohol.

Red Meat

After eating a lot of red meat (whether it's delicious bris or juicy steaks), most of us have undone the buttons on our jeans and let the sleepiness cause inflammation. The problem is that red meat is rich in protein and fat, making it difficult for your body to work all night. To get a deeper sleep, ideally, you want all systems to be in a calm state—meat takes longer to digest than other foods.

Adequate Sleeping Postures

You may have a sleeping position that you like, or change it from time to time. Also, if you are pregnant or have specific health problems, your sleep pattern may sometimes change. In these cases, the correct sleeping posture will have a significant impact on waking up. Are you choosing the best sleeping position based on your situation?

The wrong way of sleeping can cause or aggravate neck or back pain. It can also block the airway to the lungs, causing problems such as obstructive sleep apnea. Some studies even show that the wrong sleeping posture may cause toxins to be filtered out of the brain more slowly. Read on to learn how sleep patterns affect your health in many ways.

Sleeping on Belly

Almost 7% of people sleep on their stomachs. Sometimes this is called the prone position. It can alleviate ease by moving naked eye obstacles in the airway. However, sleeping in this position may aggravate other diseases.

When you sleep, your neck and spine are not in a neutral position. It may cause neck and back pain. Sleeping in the stomach puts pressure on the nerves and causes numbness, tingling, and neuralgia. If you are a stomach confined person, it is best to choose another sleeping position. If you can't change your habits, put your forehead on a pillow, keep your head and spine in a neutral place, and have room to breathe.

Freefall

Almost 7% of people sleep on their stomachs with their heads up. People who fall asleep in this way have their arms wrapped around or hidden under the pillow.

Sleeping on Your Back

Back sleeping also has its advantages and disadvantages. Sleep experts call this a supine position. Let's begin with the bad news. Many people who sleep on their backs may experience low back pain. It may also worsen existing back pain, so this is not the best sleeping position for low back pain. If you snooze or sleep apnea, sleeping on your back may also aggravate these conditions. Women should avoid holding this position in the later stages of pregnancy. Sleeping on your back also has health benefits. Your neck, head, and spine are generally positioned, so you are unlikely to suffer neck pain. Lying on your back with your head slightly raised on a small pillow is considered the best sleeping position for heartburn.

Soldier Position

The sleeper lies on his back with his arms down and close to the body in this position. About 8% of people sleep like this. It is a poor choice for snoring and may prevent you from falling asleep. It prevents you from getting enough rest, consults your doctor.

Starfish Position

A person sleeping in a starfish pose has his arms raised above his head and rests on his back. About 5% of people sleep in this way. Like all people who sleep back to back, people who sleep in starfish pose may be prone to ping and have sleeping problems.

Sleeping Beside You

So far, the lateral position is the most popular. Sleep scientists also refer to this as the lateral sleep position. This position may be right for those who hit more. However, if you have some form of arthritis, sleeping on your side may make you feel pain.

Curving upwards may also prevent you from breathing deeply, because doing so may restrict the diaphragm.

Side Sleep and Brain Damage

Sleeping on your side may be useful for your brain. Scientists have recently learned that our mind clears waste faster when we sleep. It is not clear whether your sleeping position will affect waste removal. But a study of rats showed that lying on the side may be more effective than other postures in removing brain waste.

Wrinkle Worry

Although bedridden people have many benefits, as they age, a disadvantage may arise. Because you push down on your face in a side position, this posture may cause facial wrinkles and cause the facial skin to swell over time.

Sagging Breasts

Women lying on their sides may find that their breast ligaments slowly stretch over time, causing their breasts to sag. It has not been scientifically proven, but it is still a concern for many people. If you have questions about this, a simple solution is to use pillows to support your breasts. Women with more massive breasts may find that a bra can provide extra support and make them sleep more comfortably.

Fetal Position

Approximately 41% of people sleep in a specific side position, with their knees bent and their sides retracted to the side. Side sleepers with bent legs and bent torso sleep in the fetal position. Some studies have shown that more women sleep in this position than men, although other studies are skeptical. It may be the right choice for pregnant women because this posture can improve the mother and fetus's blood circulation. If sleeping in this way hurts your hips, placing a pillow between your knees may relieve stress

Log Location

A person sleeping in a log posture has his arms down beside his body and rests on his side. About 15% of people sleep like wood. When sniffing, this sleeping position may be right for you, but you may wake up painfully if you have arthritis.

Annual Position

The person who desires to sleep lies on his side with his arms extended in front of his body. If you have difficulty breathing while sleeping, your posture may be right, but your posture may belong. About 13% of people sleep in this position.

Spoon Position

The spoon is the couple's side-lying position; the person in the back row brings the person in the front row close to their body. Like other poses, this pose has its advantages and disadvantages. As for the disadvantages, couples may fall asleep in this way more frequently because you are more likely to be lived by your partner. However, the spoon can also be hugged to stimulate the release of oxytocin. It is a hormone that promotes bonding, reduces stress, and helps you fall asleep faster. Just embracing for 10 minutes is enough to trigger the release of oxytocin.

Which Party Is Best For GERD?

Believe it or not, knowing the best sleep habits can reduce the symptoms of acid reflux. Sleeping on the right side may cause more acid to leak through the esophagus. Sleeping on the stomach or back can also make GERD symptoms worse. To reduce the risk of GERD problems, patients usually sleep best on the left side. People with congestive heart disease avoid sleeping on their back and left side.

Side Sleep and Heart Failure

People with congestive heart disease avoid sleeping on their back and left side. Their heartbeat may interfere with sleep in these positions. These patients tend to sleep on the right side.

Sleeping on the right side can protect people with heart failure from further health damage.

The Best Sleeping Posture for Sleep Apnea and Snoring

To minimize the risk of hitting, it is usually best to sleep on your side. Sleeping on your back may aggravate the snoring nor, but for fewer hitters, sleeping on the back can make them feel more relaxed the next day.

Tips to Stop Playing Nor

If you sniff, but still want to sleep on your back, try putting some pillows under your head to reduce sniffing risk. If snoring arises you up, or if you gasp or feel tired when you wake up during the day, it's time to see a doctor.

Sleep Apnea

Severe or snoring may be a sign of sleep apnea because the airway is blocked, causing you to stop breathing and start breathing during sleep. Sleep apnea is related to high blood pressure, heart disease, and stroke. If you suffer from apnea, it is well known that the way you sleep will affect your sleepiness the next day. A large study found that most patients with obstructive sleep apnea sleep better on their side, have fewer sleep interruptions, and spend more time awake the next day. However, the same study found that when people with severe

OSA went to bed the next day, they fell asleep compared to their backs. If you think you may have OSA, ask your doctor for sleep advice.

The Best Sleeping Position for Back, Shoulder, and Neck Pain

If you face back pain, sleeping on your stomach or back may worsen the problem. Switch to sleeping on your side to minimize the risk of back pain. To further relieve the pain, put a pillow between your knees to keep your hips aligned. If you have to sleep on your back, placing a pillow under your knees will reduce your back pressure. Pain in shoulders, neck, and upper back is hurtful.

While sleeping, arthritis and other painful conditions of the upper spine may worsen or improve. However, research on what position is ideal seems to be inconsistent. A large study found that people who sleep on starfish have less shoulder pain, with the back of their hands on the chest or near their head, and their backs on the starfish. But this cannot explain whether these people's sleep patterns alleviated their shoulder pain, or whether their pain eased and caused them to sleep. A later study found that people who sleep with their arms facing both sides (soldier posture) less activate the shoulder muscles to reduce shoulder pain.

Best Sleeping Positions during Pregnancy

Side Sleep

Doctors usually advise you to sleep on your side during pregnancy, especially over time. Why is this so? It boils down to blood flow.

Left: During pregnancy, try to sleep on the left side is often referred to as the "ideal" situation. Placing yourself on your body's left side allows the inferior vena cava (IVC) to get the best blood flow, which is a large vein that runs parallel to your right spine. It delivers blood to your heart and then to your baby. Sleeping on the left side can also decrease the pressure on the liver and kidneys. It means that there is more room for regular operation, which helps solve the swelling of hands, ankles, and feet.

Right: Therefore, if the most ideal is the left-should, you avoid the right? Unnecessary. The 2019 research review shows that both left and right sleeping have the same safety. When you sleep on the right, there is a small risk of IVC compression problems, but it depends on where you are most relaxed.

Ways to Make Side Sleep Work

If you are not sleeping on the side, here are some suggestions to make you feel more natural or comfortable. If you are particularly worried about your sleeping posture, you can even ask your partner to check your condition from time to time to help you put it in a better posture.

The First Three Months: Generally, you can sleep in any position at any time. However, if you want to develop a habit of preferring yourself, try merely sliding the pillow between your legs. When making adjustments, this can reduce discomfort in the hips and lower body. And, if you want to be a little better, you can consider using an orthopedic knee pillow made of memory foam.

Mid-Term: As your abdomen grows, you need to make sure that the mattress is firm to avoid bending your back. If your bed is too soft, you can consider sliding a plank between the bed and the spring. You may also need to research pregnancy pillows. They are U-shaped or C-shaped and are wrapped around your entire body to help sleep on your side. When placing the cushion, the pad should travel along your back and hug the front part while sliding between your knees.

Late: Continue to use pregnancy pillows as support. If you find that the abdomen is getting heavier and heavier, study the wedge pillow. You can paste them under and behind the stomach to prevent rolling. If you are not used to lying on your side, try using a pad to support your upper body at a 45-degree angle. In this way, your back will not be flat, and the compression force can be released from the IVC. Also, you can try to lift a few inches of books or blocks on the bed.

Belly Sleeping

Want to know if you can sleep on your stomach during pregnancy? You can definitely—at least for a while. You won't be able to sleep in your stomach until about 16 to 18 weeks. At that time, your bumps may become more significant, making this posture less and less ideal. It might be a bit like you are going to sleep on a watermelon. In addition to comfort, if you feel an upset stomach for some reason, there is no need to worry. The uterine wall and amniotic fluid protect the baby from being squeezed.

To make this position more comfortable, you can consider buying a stomach sleeping pillow. Some are inflatable, some are more like sturdy pillows, with a large incision for your abdomen. No matter which method you choose, the idea is to keep your eyes closed while giving your baby (and you) enough breathing space.

Go Back to Sleep

It is generally considered safe to sleep on the back during the first three months. After that, you may have heard of sleeping on a stillborn baby all night. Before you worry too much, please understand that the research is small, and there may be other factors, such as sleep apnea or recall bias. Similarly, some experts point out that this may be just sleeping on your back all night, which is dangerous, and it is almost impossible for all the restroom trips and insomnia you may encounter.

These studies cannot be discounted entirely. Finally, sleeping in bed may reduce your risk of stillbirth by 5.8% after 28 weeks. Also, there are other problems with supine. This posture may cause back pain, hemorrhoids, digestive problems, and low blood circulation. It may make you feel dizzy. Are you worried about waking up in the middle of the night? Probably not, but it is a good idea to try other positions. If your sleeper is relatively stable (lucky you!) and you often find yourself on your back, consider placing a wedge pillow behind you. This way, when you try to roll back, you will stop at a certain angle to allow the blood to continue to flow and provide nutrition for your baby.

The Best Sleeping Position for Back Pain

Back pain not only prevents you from getting a good night's sleep, but the current problem can be made worse by a good night's sleep. Poor sleep can also be a significant cause of back pain. It is because some positions can put unnecessary pressure on the neck, hips, and back. It is essential to manage the natural curvature of the spine while lying in bed. One can make sure that the head, shoulders, and hips are connected and that the back is adequately supported. It is usually the best way to sleep in a bed.

However, many people lie comfortably on their backs or find that it will make them sniff. Everyone sleeps differently, so there are several choices for those who want to sleep better and get rid of back pain. People who suffer from back pain at night try the following currencies, and the technique can be skipped.

Lie on Your Back with Your Knees Bent

Lying flat is generally considered to be the best sleep for a healthy back. As such, the weight is evenly distributed over the entire length of the human body's largest surface. It also reduces pressure points and ensures a good arrangement of the head, neck, and spine. Having a small pillow under the knee can be extra helpful. It can help maintain the natural curvature of the spine. To adapt to this sleeping position, one must:

- Lie flat on your back to the ceiling and avoid turning your head.

- Keep pillows to support your head and neck.

- Put a small pillow under your knees.

Use a Pillow to Lie on Your Side between Your Knees

Although lying on the side is a common and healthy sleeping position, it can push the spine out of place. It will suppress the back. It's easy to fix. Whoever is leaning against can lean on knees. It will elevate the thighs and restore the natural alignment of the hips, pelvis, and spine. To adapt to this sleeping position, one must:

- Go to bed and carefully roll to the side.
- Keep pillows to support your head and neck.
- Stretch your knees slightly, and place a pillow between them.

For extra support, use more pillows, especially on the waist, to fill the space between the body and the mattress. People accustomed to sleeping in front can also try to place a large pillow against their chest and abdomen to help them sleep and keep their back straight.

Sleep as a Fetus

For people with intervertebral disc herniation, the condition of the curled fetus can be relieved at night. It is because lying on the side of the knee on the knee can reduce the rotation of the spine and help to open the joints. To adapt to this sleeping position, one must:

- Go to bed and carefully roll to the side.

- Keep pillows to support your head and neck.

- Stretch your knees toward your chest until your back is relatively straight.

Sleep in Front, With a Pillow under Your Stomach

Lying on the face of the body is generally considered the worst sleep position. However, for those who have difficulty sleeping in a different position, a thin pillow under the abdomen and hips may improve spinal alignment. Sleeping on the front can also benefit people with herniated or digested discs. To adapt to this sleeping position, one must:

- Go to bed and lie down in front of them.

- Place a thin pillow below the abdomen and hips to lift the middle.

- Use a plain pillow for your head or consider not falling asleep.

Sleeping Down in Front

Another reason to think of front sleep as insufficient is that the head is usually to one side. It twists the spine and puts extra pressure on the neck, shoulders, and back. To avoid this, try to lie face down. You lean against your forehead and give yourself room to breathe. You can use a tiny bit hard pillow or a hard-rolled towel. In addition to resting under the abdomen, it should also be done. To adapt to this sleeping position, one must:

- Go to bed and roll in front of them.

- Place a thin pillow under the abdomen and hips to lift the middle.

Place a pillow or rolled towel under your forehead to have plenty of breathing space between your mouth and the mattress.

Sleep on Your Back

Sleeping on your back can be helpful for back pain, especially for people with spondylolisthesis. If you find that resting on a reconnector is a great relief, it is worth investing in an adjustable bed that can be positioned accordingly.

Baby Sleeping Position

Babies fall asleep a lot, and it is essential to ensure that they sleep in a safe position, because the wrong sleeping position of babies can sometimes cause SIDS (Sudden Infant Death Syndrome). SIDS in children is caused by asphyxiation or strangulation. If you have a baby at home, you must know everything about the baby's ideal sleeping position and how certain sleeping positions can cause sudden neonatal death.

You may have observed babies sleeping in different positions. Some of these sleeping positions increase the risk of Sudden Infant Death (SUDI). SUDI is a broad term that covers all premature infant deaths, including small island developing States, which are usually caused by asphyxia of the newborn. Sleeping on the chest/abdomen is one of the most dangerous positions for babies. Let's look at more sleeping positions, which increase the risk of SUDI.

Stomach Sleeping Position

The sleeping position on the baby's belly is very unsafe for the following reasons:

This position may pressure the baby's jaw and block the airway, making it difficult for the baby to breathe. Sleeping on the stomach will bring the baby's face very close to the bedsheet, allowing him to breathe the same air. It may result in breathing circulating air with low oxygen content. Sleeping on a very soft mattress may cause the baby to suffocate. When lying on a soft bed, the risk of exhalation is higher because the baby's face extends more in-depth into the mattress's soft fabric. It may block the baby's airway in various ways.

Also, since the nose is very close to the mattress in this position, the baby will eventually breathe the microorganisms present in the bedsheet covering the bed, which may cause allergies. Sometimes, under certain medical conditions, the doctor may advise parents to place the baby on the stomach where it sleeps. Generally, it is recommended that children with gastroesophageal reflux or specific upper respiratory tract malformations (such as Pierre Robin syndrome) fall asleep in this position, but they may not work correctly. Therefore, it is recommended to consult a doctor correctly before putting the baby to sleep.

Sleep on Your Side

It is not recommended to sleep on the baby's side because the baby will eventually roll onto the belly while asleep, which increases the risk of SIDS due to one of the reasons mentioned above. So, which sleeping position is right for your baby? Well, now the only option left is the supine sleeping position. Let's take a closer look.

Safe Sleeping Position for Babies

The back-sleeping state is the safest and best sleeping position for babies. For babies, this is the most recommended sleeping position because it keeps the airway open and minimizes choking risk. The National Institute of Child Health and Human Development (NICHD) recommends naps and backrest positions for babies to maintain good sleep throughout the night.

Children who lie on their backs for a long time may have "positional plagiocephaly" (flat head), or babies may have "head and neck deformity" (flat back). However, these are temporary conditions; once the baby changes, they will return to normal. That being said, there are some tricks you can use to avoid these situations altogether:

- The baby has more tummy time when he is awake.
- Lay the baby on his side when he is not asleep.
- Reduce time spent on transport vehicles or car seats.
- These techniques allow babies to lie down in different positions instead of lying on the back.

The Secret to Safe Baby Sleep

Here are some tips to reduce SUDI's risk and ensure that your baby has a good sleep.

Use a Firm Mattress in The Crib

Many parents mistakenly choose soft baby mattresses. This situation must be avoided. The baby must sleep on a sturdy bed. You must also avoid using bumpers, pillows, or stuffed toys in the crib because it may accidentally cover the baby's head.

Avoid Quilts

Avoid using quilts on top of the mattress to make the quilt soft. It may cause the baby to sink under the bedding and increase the risk of suffocation. Just place a clean, suitable mattress in the crib and cover it with a clean sheet, which is enough to give your baby a good night's sleep.

Pull the Blanket Correctly

The blanket can only cover the baby's chest. The arms must be placed outside the mantle to ensure that the blanket does not roll over the head and choke the baby. You can use sleeping bags with neck and armpits easily available in the market and highly recommended. They are safe to use and can also keep babies warm.

Pajamas Should Be Light Clothes

For the baby to sleep well, it is important to wear light clothes. Make sure the clothes are not too tight or loose.

Keep the Room Cool at Night

It is also recommended that children sleep in a cool environment, preferably at 20 degrees Celsius.

Use A Pacifier When Necessary

It is giving babies a pacifier before going to bed. However, it is not recommended to force newborn babies to use a pacifier. Wait until they are about four weeks old before trying.

Avoid Sleeping with Babies

It is not recommended for babies to sleep with their parents, siblings, or even twins. Sleeping with babies can increase opportunities for small island developing states. When sleeping, arms, or breasts or clothes may accidentally cover the baby's face, eventually suffocating the baby to death. Sleeping with babies is a common habit in India because it is easy to feed babies at night. But now you know why it must be avoided!

Share the Same Room

The crib must be installed in the same room as the parents. It can facilitate breastfeeding, and it is easy for parents to pay close attention to the baby's sleeping position. The AAP (American Academy of Pediatrics) recommends room-sharing rather than bed-sharing as a safety guide for babies' sleep.

Chapter 4. Create an Ideal Sleeping Environment

Organize the Room

Keeping the bedroom tidy and eliminating possible distractions is essential for your body to begin to relax. Important work documents, busy artwork, and even treadmills are all examples of stress, reminding you of the responsibility of being distracted while sleeping. Instead, try to keep your room tidy and minimally decorated.

Reduce Exposure

Try using darkroom curtains, thick curtains, or blindfolds to eliminate natural light to get an ideal sleeping environment. Light can come from anywhere—street lights, corridors, even the moon and stars—all of which will make your brain mistake it for daytime. Blue light exposure can also affect the quality of your sleep. Studies have shown that blue light irradiation can increase alertness, change the circadian rhythm, and inhibit the sleep-promoting hormone melatonin, thereby keeping you awake. When you want to put down the signal, please set the alarm for one hour so that it is time to give up the device and start going to bed or reading. You can even consider wearing filter glasses around the clock to avoid eye strain while looking at the computer or phone screen.

Use Essential Oils

No wonder smell affects how we feel by associating the scent with emotion and memory. Sleep essential oils that are often overlooked can help you relax and eventually subside. Aromatherapy with essential oils is a quick and inexpensive solution to eliminate sleep deprivation and help you relax. Lavender and vanilla are the most popular oils that can help you fall asleep. They can be added to an aroma diffuser or evaporator and dispersed in the bedroom.

Emphasize the Symmetry of Furniture Placement

For a better sleeping environment, your furniture's location must be considered because it plays a vital role in the bedroom's function and symmetry. For the best balance, place your bed as close as possible to the middle of the wall, and leave space on both sides. When lying on the bed, your feet should be close to the entrance, facing the door. If possible, try to avoid laying your head under the window.

Find Your Ideal Pillow

To keep your spine straightened while you sleep, the usual rule of thumb is to change your pillow every 1 to 2 years. However, if you cannot stay comfortable after waking up or wake up with headaches, neck pain, and shoulder pain, you can consider finding a replacement earlier. When choosing pillow hardness, you should keep your sleeping posture in mind from softer choices (such as down pillows) to healthier options (such as buckwheat pillows). Stomach sleepers tend to choose thinner pads, back sleepers think medium support is best, and side sleepers tend to choose thicker pillows. If you have allergies or asthma, you can select a hypoallergenic covering to prevent any allergens that may cause symptoms.

Invest in a New Mattress

It is also essential to consider your sleeping position, as this will determine whether a soft bed or a firm bed is the right choice for you. No matter what kind of mattress you use (maybe memory foam, natural fiber, or hot and cold mattress), be sure to test the store's options. Even mail-order mattress firms offer free home trials. Although most beds have a life span of up to 10 years, the upfront cost is daunting. If your financial situation is not right, you can add foam topping to the mattress to increase comfort and help prevent stiffness and itching. Some beds are designed with specific health conditions in mind, so if you suffer from sleep apnea, sciatica, scoliosis, etc., please consult your doctor when choosing a new mattress.

Use the Sleeping Robot

If stress and anxiety hit your ability to fall asleep, then the world's first sleep robot can support you calm your mind and relax your body. The robot is equipped with calm music, which can replicate the breathing rhythm and fit your chest naturally to enhance comfort and security. Now you can subconsciously adjust the breathing pattern to slow down and synchronize with the robot, thus relaxing and falling asleep quickly.

Consider a New Worksheet

When you wander around the sheets, you will find several different threads counts, weaves, and chosen materials. These all add to the bedsheets' warmth and softness, and the choice of the ideal bed sheet depends on the type of sleeper you use. Although covering you endlessly, do you still wake up shaking in the middle of the night? Popular choices for fighting the cold are wool and knitwear, followed by silk. Or maybe you wake up as if you were sleeping in a sauna. Suppose it sounds like you, consider researching materials like cotton and linen, and perhaps even bamboo sheets. Designed specifically for "heat pillows," the breathable and temperature-regulating bed sheets reduce heat dissipation and help you fall asleep all night.

Find the Ideal Bedspread

From bedspreads and duvet covers to blankets and quilts, the top layers come in many different styles. These top layers can add more warmth and style to your bed. Each kind of bed cover provides different levels of weight and texture, and what affects your sleeping environment and comfort is entirely up to you.

Use Audio Equipment/Air Conditioning

If you have a partner who sniffs, lives on a busy street, or loses your mind, then the white noise sleep machine may be what you lack. Light sleepers may prefer applications that provide various natural noises, such as ocean waves or light rain. Or, a simple bedroom fan can bring discomfort to purely quiet people.

Change Your View of The Room

One of the most significant ways to associate a place with it is to maximize the room's sleep efficiency. Ideally, your room should only be used for two purposes: sleep and romance. All other things done in the place serve no other purpose and can only distract your sleep time. But how can you improve your room so that it is exclusively related to sleep?

Clean-Up All the Debris

Your bedroom is not your gym, office, or game room. To start associating it with sleep, you need to clear everything that can cause distractions. Put the treadmill in another room, get rid of the computer and desk, and most importantly (and probably the most difficult) the TV. Using the bedroom as a place for other activities will only cause your brain to associate the room with other things. If your bedroom is near the office, it can make your mind busy and even anxious about work because you associate it with busy work.

Getting rid of the TV helps a lot. On the one hand, it is easy to watch before going to bed because it is in the room. When you are addicted to the story, participating in the show can make your mind clearer. The TV also emits blue light, which may induce the body to slow down melatonin production. Light is related to awakening. When there is sufficient light, your body does not produce so much melatonin, which is a hormone that promotes sleep and makes falling asleep more difficult.

Throw Away All Electronic Equipment

For the same logic, you should not have a TV or computer in your bedroom, nor should you have a cell phone, tablet, laptop, portable game console, or e-reader in the room. Most of these devices also emit sleep stealing light and are used to consume content that might entice you to fall asleep because it is so attractive. You should also adjust the position of the alarm clock. Not just is the light from the digital representation distracting people's attention. Still, many people find themselves continually checking the time displayed on the clock. If it is too late, they begin to worry about losing sleep. Worry about lack of sleep can cause anxiety, which can lead to more sleep loss. The best solution for an alarm clock is to set the alarm clock at a given wake-up time, place it on the other side of the room, and then move it away. It saves you from worrying about time and can also prevent you from falling asleep by pressing the snooze button because it will force you to get up in the morning to turn it off.

Paint the Room

The color of the bedroom will affect the amount of sleep you get. A survey of more than 2,000 British houses found that blue, yellow, and green can help sleepers get the most sleep time. Blue averages 7 hours and 52 minutes, yellow averages 7 hours 40 minutes, and green averages 7 hours 36 minutes. These colors are usually associated with calmness and relaxation and can help you relax when you are trying to rest.

At the second end of the spectrum, colors such as purple, brown, and gray can disrupt the amount of sleep you get. The average hours of these colors are 6 hours and 12 minutes for gray, 6 hours and 5 minutes for brown, and 5 hours and 56 minutes for purple. Theory suggests that purple is an artistic color that can stimulate creativity. At the same time, brown and gray are usually associated with dullness and depression.

Color has a significant influence on our mood and can affect our sleep quality by creating a calm environment. Studies have shown that the best bedroom sleep color is blue, followed by yellow, green, and silver. Try to stick to neutral, soft, or soft shadows, because bold colors will trick the brain into thinking it needs to be wary.

As you know, many things can make you lose sleep. Fortunately, most of these items can be solved by maintaining good sleep hygiene and prioritizing sleep. Unfortunately, good sleep hygiene and a maximized sleep environment do not always help them sleep better. Many people suffer from sleep disorders and need to be diagnosed and treated, starting with sleep research.

Make Your Room Quiet

If you live in a noisy neighborhood or have loud neighbors in your apartment, this may cost some work. In lighter sleep stages, you are more likely to be awakened, but your brain will make sounds during sleep even if you are not awake. Studies have shown that exposure to noise at night may increase the risk of cardiovascular disease. There are several steps you can take to quiet the bedroom and reduce exposure to outside sounds:

- Install sound-absorbing curtains. These materials are usually a bit thicker than ordinary curtains.

- Using a fabric headboard helps to absorb the sound of the room.

- Use a white noise machine or app in your room, which is the right choice if you live in a noisy area.

Place objects in your room to absorb and deflect sound. If you have ever been in an empty building, the reason for hearing such a strong echo is that the sound is deflected from the walls, floor, and ceiling, because nothing can absorb or deflect the sound. Adding items such as plants, carpets or rugs, artwork, and cabinets will reduce the number of sound waves that bounce from one plane to another.

Hang the soundproof foam sheet on the wall and ceiling, or hang it from the top. A cheaper way to do this is to build a small wooden square, place a piece of foam in the inner cloth store, and cover it with any colored cloth you like. You can hang several pictures.

If you want to see how much the sound quality of entering the room has improved, please play music at a specific volume (for example, stereo level 5) before making the change, and then perform the same operation after the change. If it improves, you must turn up the stereo to achieve the same decibel level as the current deflected and absorbed sound.

Find the Best Mattress for You

One of the most common problems people encounter when using beds is that they are old, so dented, and do not give you enough support. Most mattresses need to be replaced every 7-10 years, although this depends on the type of bed you are using.

Another problem is that the mattress is too small. If you and your partner have many pillows and bump into each other, then maybe it's time to consider a king-size bed. Also, please make sure that your mattress absorbs your partner's movement to not interfere with each other at night. It is also essential to find the right firmness for you and your partner. One way to see this is to sleep on a softer or harder mattress than the mattress. If you find that you wake up in another bed and feel better, you may need to investigate other mattresses. Many online mattress retailers will offer you a 100-day money-back guarantee for you to try their mattresses.

The last mattress issue is heating. Foam mattresses compress and therefore do not allow heat to escape from the body. There are several options to remedy a hot bed. One is to buy a new mattress. You can purchase traditional spring mattresses, which are usually not so soft but can increase air circulation. Or, you can choose a bed that combines gel and foam. You can also purchase a cooling device to circulate the cooling water through the mattress cover throughout the night, such as Chili Pad, which costs about $500. You can start with a cheaper option and buy a cool mattress cover, such as one made of bamboo or wool.

Create a Perfect Sleeping Environment for Your Baby

Enter "Baby Sleep" in Google, and an astonishing 274 million entries will appear. Yes-millions. It gives you an idea of how stressful and sleep-deprived moms are looking for something to help their newborns fall asleep. As a new parent, it is essential to understand that every baby is different. Some will sleep longer, while others will not.

Establish Routine Procedures as Early as Possible

Newborns babies have no concept of day or night and do not know when they should wake up or fall asleep earlier—they only know when they are hungry and when they are not. By establishing a calm night routine, you can help them understand that the night is relaxing and sleep. A quiet, soothing bath, followed by a baby massage and hug before going to bed, may help.

Darken Room

Shading blinds can be beneficial, especially in the hot summer, and when the sun is still shining on the baby at bedtime. Some babies sleep best when it's dark at night (even during the day), and blackout blinds can be easily bought anywhere from IKEA to Pottery Barn Kids (i.e., parents desperately anywhere may seek relief!)

Don't Be Too Quiet

Newborn babies tend to tip their feet. However, it is not necessary. Some babies sleep much better when there is background noise around. Remember, the womb sounds are not silent—before your baby is born, he is nodding to listen to your heartbeat, digestion, and silent sounds outside your body. If your baby likes unique sounds, you can try a free app called "Sleepy Sounds." Some babies may like "heavy rain," while others nod their heads to indicate "vacuum." No matter what you do, right?

Minimize Instructions

When your partner comes home late from getting off work, now decide the best time to sing "Old McDonald's" in the style of Bruce Springsteen while playing the baby's face with jazz, politely reminding them that now may not be the best time. Make a clear distinction between "sleep time" and "playtime." It is best to minimize the stimulation before going to bed, which means that before turning off the TV, dim the lights, and keep the pitch of these programs for at least half an hour, and then put it down.

Talk to Your Baby Quietly

When you dress your baby to sleep, speaking quietly with your baby may calm him down. Never underestimate the understanding of your little ones. You will be surprised by what they absorb. Every night, when you put them in the crib or shake them to sleep, saying "good night, a mother loves you" is a good day for both parties.

Healthy Habits, Let You Sleep Well

Choose the Ideal Sleep Temperature. The best temperature for a healthy night is usually between 60- and 67- degrees Fahrenheit. However, this varies from person to person, and other factors in the environment (such as climatic conditions, type of bedding, and pajamas) may affect your optimal sleep temperature. Some people sleep hotter than others, which also affects their ideal sleep temperature. Nevertheless, temperatures above 75 degrees Fahrenheit and below 54 degrees Fahrenheit will interfere with your sleep.

Avoid Sleeping with Pets. You may think that your pet is a family, so why not share a bed with them? 45% of Americans allow their dogs to lie in bed, but this may cause your restless nights. Many people are allergic to cats and dogs, and they get worse when sharing beds. These allergens can remain in clothes, pillows, and bedding and may cause reactions. Consider using multiple styles of pet beds and crates (such as nesting beds, raised beds, or heated beds), and now consider providing other sleeping arrangements for your partner.

Avoid Caffeine After 2 Pm. We have all been there-10pm, and you can still pick up the phone from Joe that afternoon. Studies have shown that consuming caffeine even 6 hours before bed can disrupt your sleep. If you rely on the afternoon pick-up service every day, caffeine-infused stimulants may affect your sleep quality and duration. Start every day with high-caffeinated beverages, and then gradually reduce your caffeine intake throughout the morning by switching to tea or decaffeinated coffee. You must minimize caffeine completely before 2 pm.

Exercise Regularly to Improve Sleep. Not only does exercise relief endorphins, but it also helps you fall asleep faster and feel rested when you wake up. Even only 10 minutes of exercise at any time of the day can greatly improve sleep quality. Joining a local gym, meeting with a personal trainer regularly, or doing your favorite physical exercises are good ways to exercise. If your schedule is limited, you can even create a home gym to increase flexibility and convenience.

Create Night Routines. Most of us do most activities at night (such as watching TV or using the phone) can be overstimulating. By aligning with a peaceful bedtime routine, your body will recognize that it's time to go to bed, and screen time may be less attractive. Your night routine is simple, such as brushing your teeth, washing your face, flossing your teeth, and even enjoying decaffeinated bedtime tea. The options are endless, and how you choose ultimately depends on you. Dim the lights, and relax.

Avoid Taking Naps Near at Night. Although naps are encouraged and provide many benefits, rest in the afternoon and evening can negatively affect your sleep quality. Instead, limit the nap time from 15 to 30 minutes. It will increase your chances of waking up and make you feel rejuvenated while still falling asleep easily before going to bed. Your circadian rhythm drops between 2 pm and 3 pm. It is the best time to rest without sleeping.

Decline to Snooze the Alarm. After sleeping the alarm, you will wake up, especially if you press the snooze button multiple times, you will get more tired. You cannot reach the vital sleep level between the two alarms, which eventually confuses your brain and interrupts the natural wake-up process. If you sleep 7 to 9 hours a night, your body does not need extra sleep and can even get up on its own before the first alarm sounds. Try to gradually reduce the number of times you snooze the alarm until you wake up after the first alarm.

Better Sleep Habits

Good sleep directly changes your physical and mental health. Failure to meet the requirements may seriously damage your daytime energy, productivity, emotional balance, and even weight. However, many of us often toss and turn at night, struggling to get the sleep we need. When you wake up at 3 in the morning, getting a good night's sleep may seem like an impossible goal, but you have far more control over the quality of sleep than you might realize. Just as the way you feel when you are awake depends on your sleep at night, you can usually find a cure for your daily work.

Unhealthy habits and lifestyle choices during the day will make you toss and turn at night, adversely affecting your mood, brain and heart health, immune system, creativity, vitality, and weight. However, by trying the following tips, you can enjoy better sleep at night, enhance your health, and develop your thinking and feeling during the day.

Keep Your Body's Natural Sleep-Wake Cycle

Keeping pace with the body's natural sleep-wake process or circadian rhythm is essential for improving sleep quality. If you maintain a regular sleep-wake-up schedule, even if you only change your sleep schedule for one or two hours, you will feel refreshed and energetic than sleeping at the same time at different times. Try to fall asleep and get up at the same time every day. It helps to set the body's internal clock and optimize sleep quality. Choose a bedtime when you usually feel tired, so as not to toss and turn. If you have enough sleep, you should wake up normally without an alarm. If you want an alarm clock, you may need to fall asleep earlier.

Avoid Sleeping, Even on Weekends. The difference in your sleep schedule on weekends, and the more jet lag-like symptoms you will experience. If you need to make up for the night, choose a daytime nap instead of sleeping. It allows you to pay off your sleep debts without disturbing your natural sleep awakening rhythm.

Be Wary of Naps. Although naps are a great way to make up for lack of sleep, if you cannot fall asleep at night, naps can worsen. Limit your nap time from 15 to 20 minutes.

Eliminate Sleepiness After Meals. If you feel sleepy before going to bed, get off the sofa and do something irritating, such as washing dishes, calling a friend, or preparing clothes for the next day. If you succumb to drowsiness, you may wake up late at night and have difficulty falling asleep.

Control Your Light Exposure

Melatonin is a natural hormone controlled by the light that helps regulate the sleep-wake cycle. In the dark, the brain will secrete more melatonin, making you tired; in the darkness, the mind will secrete more melatonin, making you more alert. However, many features of modern life can change your body's production of melatonin and change your circadian rhythm.

- **Day:** Expose yourself to fresh sunlight in the morning. The closer you wake up, the better. For example, drinking coffee outside or having breakfast by the sunny window. The light on your face can help you wake up. During the day, spend more time outside. Take a break to work in the sun during the day instead of at night, exercise, or walk the dog outdoors. Let as much natural light enter your house or work area as possible. Please keep the curtains and blinds open during the day, and try to move the desk closer to the window. If necessary, use a light therapy box. It can simulate sunlight and is especially useful in short winters.

- **In the Evening:** Avoid bright screens within 1-2 hours of bedtime. Blue light emitted by mobile phones, tablets, computers, or TVs is incredibly destructive. You can reduce the impact by using a smaller screen device, turning down the brightness, or using dimming software such as f.lux. Say no to late-night TV. The light from TV not only suppresses melatonin, but many programs are stimulating rather than relaxing. Try listening to music or audiobooks. Do not use backlight devices to read. Backlit tablets are more destructive than e-readers without their light source.

When sleeping, assured the room is dark. Use heavy curtains or shadows to block the light from the windows, or try a sleeping mask. You can also consider covering electronic devices that emit light. If you get up at night, please keep the lights off. If you want some light to move around carefully, try installing a dim night light or using a small flashlight in the hall or bathroom. It will make it easier for you to fall asleep.

Exercise During the Day

People who exercise routinely sleep better at night and restless during the day. Regular exercise can also improve the symptoms of insomnia and sleep apnea, and increase the time you spend in the restorative sleep phase. The more intensive the training, the stronger the effect of sleep; however, even light exercise (such as walking only 10 minutes a day) can improve sleep quality. You may need to spend several months of regular activities to play the role of promoting sleep fully. So be patient and concentrate on developing a persistent exercise habit.

To Sleep Better, Please Exercise Your Time Correctly. Exercise can speed up metabolism, raise body temperature, and stimulate hormones such as cortisol. It is not a problem if you exercise in the morning or afternoon, but being too close to the bed can interfere with sleep. Try to complete moderate to vigorous exercise at least three hours before bed. If you still have trouble sleeping, please exercise earlier. Relaxing low-impact activities, such as yoga or gentle stretching exercises at night, can help promote sleep.

Have a Particular Understanding of Diet?

Eating habits during the day will affect your sleep quality, especially a few hours before going to bed.

Limit caffeine and nicotine. You may be surprised to find that caffeine can cause sleep problems up to ten to twelve hours after drinking coffee! Similarly, smoking is another stimulus that may disrupt your sleep, especially if you smoke close to bedtime. Avoid large meals at night. Try to eat dinner in the evening and avoid eating a lot of fatty food within two hours of bed. Spicy or acidic foods can cause stomach upset and heartburn.

Avoid drinking alcohol before going to bed. Although a nightcap can help you relax, it will interfere with your sleep cycle after going out. Avoid drinking too much liquid at night. Drinking plenty of water may result in frequent visits to the bathroom throughout the night. Reduce sugary foods and refined carbohydrates. Eating many sugar and refined carbohydrates during the day, such as white bread, white rice, and pasta, may cause wakefulness at night, allowing you to escape deep and restorative sleep.

Night Snacks Can Help You Fall Asleep. For some people, eating snacks before bed can promote sleep. For others, eating before going to bed can cause indigestion and make sleep more difficult. If you need a bedtime snack, please try:

- Half a turkey sandwich
- A small bowl of whole wheat low-sugar cereals
- Milk or yogurt
- A banana

Slow Down and Clean Your Head

Do you often find yourself weak to fall asleep or wake up every night? The residual stress, worry, and anger of your day can make it difficult for you to fall asleep. Taking steps to control your overall stress level and learning how to curb your anxiety habits can help you relax at night. You can also try to promote relaxing bedtime habits to help you prepare for sleep, such as practicing relaxation techniques, taking a hot bath or dimming the lights, and listening to light music or audiobooks.

The problem of cleaning your head at night may also stem from your daytime habits. During the day, your brain is overstimulated, so it becomes more difficult to relax at night. Maybe like many of us, you often interrupt your task of checking your phone, email, or social media during the day. Then, when you want to fall asleep at night, your brain has become accustomed to seeking new stimuli, so it becomes difficult to relax. Help yourself by setting aside specific times of the day to check your phone and social media, and focus as much as possible on completing a task. You will be able to rest at ease when you go to bed.

Deep Breathing Activities Can Support You Fall Asleep. Breathing from the belly instead of the chest can activate the relaxation response and lower your heart rate, blood pressure, and stress level, thereby helping you fall asleep.

- Lie on the bed and close your eyes.

- Place one hand on your chest and the other hand on your stomach.

- Breathe through the nose. The hand on the belly should be raised. The hands on the chest should barely move.

- Exhale through your mouth, expelling as much air as possible while contracting the abdominal muscles. When you exhale, your hand on your stomach should move inwards, but your other hand should move very little.

- Continue breathing through the nose and breathing through the mouth. Inhale as much as possible to make the lower abdomen rise and fall. Count as you exhale.

Body Scanning Exercise Can Help You Fall Asleep. By concentrating your attention on various parts of your body, you can determine where the pressure or tension is exposed and then release it.

- Lie on your back, cross your legs, relax your sides, and close your eyes tightly. Focus on breathing for about two minutes until you start to feel relaxed.

- Turn your attention to the toes of your right foot. Pay attention to any tension while continuing to focus on breathing. Imagine that every deep breath flow to the toes. Stay focused on the area for at least three to five seconds.

- Move the focus to the right sole. Adjust the feeling of that part of the body and imagine every breath on your feet' soles. Then move the focus to the right ankle and repeat. Move to the calf, knee, thigh, buttocks, and repeat the left leg process. From there, move your torso up through the lower back and abdomen, upper back and chest, and shoulders. Pay close attention to any part of the body that is tense.

- After completing the body scan, relax, and pay attention to your physical sensations. You should feel relaxed and can easily fall asleep.

Improve Your Sleeping Environment

A quiet bedtime routine sends a powerful signal to your brain that it is time to relax the day's stress. Sometimes even small changes in the environment can have a significant impact on the quality of your sleep. Keep your room dark, calm, and quiet:

- Reduce noise. If you can't avoid or eliminate the noise made by neighbors, traffic, or other household people, try to cover it with a fan or sound machine. Earplugs may also help.

- Keep the room cool. Most people sleep best in a cold, well-ventilated room (about 65°F or 18°C). A bedroom that is hot or cold will interfere with quality sleep.

- Make sure your bed is comfortable. Your bedspread should leave enough space for you to stretch and rotate comfortably without tangling. If you often wake up with a sore back or neck, you may want to try different degrees of mattress firmness, foam tops, and pillows that provide more or less support.

- Reserve a bed for sleeping and love. By not operating, watching TV, or using your phone, tablet, or computer while lying in bed, your brain connects the bedroom with sleep and sex, making it easier to relax at night.

Learn How to Fall Asleep Again

It is normal to wake up briefly at night, but if you have trouble falling asleep, these tips may help:

Don't worry about doing your best, and don't overemphasize that you can't fall asleep again, because this kind of pressure will only keep your body awake. To keep your mind clear, focus on the sensations of the body, or practice breathing exercises. Take a breath, then exhale as you say or think about the word "Ahhh." Take another breath and repeat.

The goal is relaxation, not sleep. If you find it difficult to fall asleep, try a relaxation method such as visualization, progressive muscle relaxation, or meditation, which can be made without even getting up. Even if it cannot replace sleep, relaxation can still help your body rejuvenate. Perform quiet, non-stimulating activities. If you wake up for more than 15 minutes, get up, and engage in peaceful, non-stimulating activities, such as reading. Keep the light dim and avoid blocking the screen, so as not to remind the body that it is time to wake up.

Postpone worry and brainstorming. If you feel a little upset when you wake up at night, please make a short note on paper and postpone the concern about the problem until the next day to be resolved. Similarly, if you have a good idea to keep you awake, please write a note on the paper and then fall asleep, because you know that your work efficiency will be significantly improved after a good night's sleep.

Chapter 5. Positive Affirmations for Better Sleep

Imagine closing your eyes at the end of a long day without being stressed. How happy are the spirit, body, and soul when you wake up in the morning? You need that! You deserve a rest. Using these active bedtimes will lead you into a calm state of mind so that your body gets the rest it deserves. I have worked my best today, and I am willing to forgive others. My best is forever good enough, and everything else is worth forgiving. I am ready to try this belief: I have tried my best. I ignore the rest. It's time to let go.

Everything Is Fine, and I Got Support

I don't need to figure out everything—not all at once, and not tonight. My question is attracted by the silent night. I believe that everything I need will be presented to me, cleanly and clearly. Currently, sleep is the best.

There Is a Kind of Relaxation in the Air

Every time I breathe in my abdomen, a peaceful trick flows and makes me spacious. A faint sense of joy floated on me. A kind of calm consciousness eliminates all worries. My forehead has become soft. Now, sleep has become easier for me.

I Believe Everything Is Possible

I do my best. I don't need to view the entire path. When I have to adjust, I can. When I have to let go, I can learn how to do it. I accept all the good things that are about to happen.

I Am Free at the Moment

I got rid of the troubles of yesterday, today, and tomorrow. This moment is purely my intention. When I sink into a profound existence, every layer of me becomes lighter. It is my home.

I Do Not Just Think That Happened

My inner thoughts don't tell me who I am, and I am more than just their information. I am the one who hears and witnesses. What a relief: thought is just thought, not me.

I Release All Negative Emotions

I loosened my restraints and plunged me into a painful identity, and I am not my pain. Negativity cannot define me. I accept the things here and free myself from all fantasies, and I get and release negative emotions to gain freedom.

When I Breathe In, I Breathe Out

Every inhalation will bring rich and beneficial energy. I use existence to inhale and find the area that needs to be released. I exhale earnestly, eliminating all tension and illness. Each exhalation brings me closer and closer to peace.

I Rest for a While

Between today and tomorrow, absolute peace rules my world. I stopped spinning, and my soul thanked my breathing space. This pause can take me in, prepared to show me how to nourish everything, one breath at a time.

I Am Very Light and Can Fall Asleep

My path to sleep is all about releasing unwanted things. The less I carry, the lighter I become. I did not add myself; I lightened the burden. Every burden I fall makes it easier for me to fall asleep.

I Am Released Today

I let go of anxiety, worry, anger, and blame. I release my anxiety and stress. I removed the weight of today and the shoulders' weight, and I let go of negative thoughts and keep happy thoughts. In my sleep, I will find the freedom to recognize happiness and peace again.

I Forgive All This

What happened is so there is no other way to make it a reality. Therefore, I leave it alone; I leave life as it is. I forgive the people, I ignore the situation, and I forgive myself. I believe in life, and I am safe.

I Have the Right to Fall Asleep

I permit myself to close my eyes tonight and wake up tomorrow to refresh me. I was allowed to sleep well. My body, mind, and soul deserve to rest. What I did today is enough. I have enough, and now I can give myself time to rest.

I Now Enter a Deep and Peaceful Sleeping Place

My bedroom is a home of peace and relaxation. When I entered this room and climbed onto the bed at night, my thoughts naturally began to soften. My burden is lightened, and sleep is almost here.

I Am Very Grateful

I am grateful for this life. I thank the people who have been my teachers. I am very thankful for the lessons experience has taught us. I appreciate the love received, given, and shared. I thank the bright day. I am grateful for the darkness of the night, and I will fall asleep in it tonight.

I Have Dreams

As the night darkened, my worries gradually faded. I fell asleep peacefully, knowing that I had done everything today. I have a dream because tomorrow will have new brilliance and new power. I fell asleep with dreams; everything is fine.

May My Sleep Be Peaceful

May my sleep be peaceful. May my dreams be filled with love, and May my soul awaken the infinite possibilities of my life's happiness.

I Ask You to Guarantee a Good Sleep Quality

I welcome peace into my home, and I invite light into my heart. Love, happiness, and comfort have always existed in my soul. My spirit is content; my mind is static. I became quiet and relaxed. I am grateful, and I welcome you to have a good sleep.

I Choose Peace

I choose peace. I closed my eyes and decided to look again with new eyes, beyond what I could see with the naked eye. Peace is my top priority. Peace begins with me; there is peace in my soul.

I Am in Harmony with the Universe

I match my heartbeat with the beating of the universe. I was in harmony with the night and sleep that followed. Now there is no separation, only one heartbeat beating slowly and calmly. Today, I do my best. There is nothing I can do now to change everything that happened.

- I am now lying in bed, free from today's stress, fear, anger, and accusation. I invite and welcome calmness and serenity. It's time for me to relax my day and get a good night's sleep to deal with what will happen tomorrow, strong and resilient.

- I believe that my body and mind know what to do. All I have to do is make it happen. I don't need to fall asleep. It will happen only when the time is up.

- I feel calm and safe in the bedroom. It is a space where I can let go, completely my own, and completely relax.

- I have nothing to do now, nowhere to go. No one needs me at the moment. It's time to care and sympathize with yourself. I should fall asleep and keep my body and mind healthy.

- I breathe slowly and calmly. I am clearing up the thoughts of busy racing. I am listening to my breathing. I am calm and sleepy.

- I am grateful for the many things that have brought me happiness and comfort in my life. I have a safe place to sleep, I have people who love me throughout my life, and I have all the internal resources needed to deal with everything I encounter.

- (Parents) Today I did my best. I didn't pay much. I take care of my children, feed them, play with them, listen to them, keep them safe, and love them. I now allow myself to close my eyes and rest.

- I relax. I am soothing my head, face, shoulders, stomach, hips, legs, and feet. I am releasing the tension in my jaw. I feel very relaxed.

- Sleeping is the most natural thing. There is no reason why I cannot sleep. Billions of people are sleeping now as if I were going to fall asleep. I fall asleep every night and will fall asleep tonight.

- Now, I can do nothing; I have nothing to do. Everything is on the list, so I can let it go. No need for my attention now.

Hypnosis for Deep Sleep

- I spent a long day and did a lot of things. It's time to go to bed. I'm tired and ready to go to bed. I was sleepy and fell asleep until I got enough sleep.

- I am over now; I let go of what happened today. I am completely at this moment, in bed. I am myself, without any association or responsibility.

- Now is the time for my deep and peaceful sleep to rejuvenate me to become strong and full of energy tomorrow. I am powerless now to help others. The best thing I can do is take a break.

- I am going to sleep, and I will stay asleep. If I wake up, it's okay, because I will fall asleep again. I believe I will get everything I need.

- I try my best to be the person I want to be, and that is enough. Everything I have done is enough. I've had enough.

- I don't need to be anywhere; no one needs me. I have completely turned off the power and disconnected from everything around me. I will not be disturbed by the surrounding noises, because they are not suitable for me and will not affect me.

- After a good night's sleep, everything to do in the morning will be better. I can do nothing now-it's time to sleep.

- I am who I am, nowhere, lying in bed. I'm free. I am relaxed and ready to sleep.

- I feel relaxed about my current life, and I believe that I will be able to move forward and make the best decision in due course.

- It would help if you had a positive reminder to remind you that you can solve all your problems without sleeping. Nothing is so important, and you can't wait until tomorrow to solve it. Taking a break may help you better solve the problems that bother you.

- I don't need to figure out everything—not all at once, and not tonight. My question is attracted by the silent night. I believe that everything I need will be presented to me, cleanly and clearly. Currently, sleep is the best.

- Everything is in the house of my soul. Everything is always good. Mistakes will be eliminated one day; before that, I was welcomed by various teachers. I develop my consciousness here. Every experience is part of this sacred process.

- Even if I fall asleep, life is being handled for me. I may not know how to complete all the work, but I am willing to believe that in the end, nothing was done. The higher order of things ensures that everything is taken care of.

- No matter how fixed the thinking mode is, I can choose again. Before other ideas that feel good persist, I am willing to show up and practice them. I am grateful for my simple intention: so sleep is easier.

- I can treat myself politely. It is a practice, and I am willing to participate. Personal struggle is also worthy of patience. I am now moving in a better direction.

- I am taller than any dark thoughts. When my body sank into the bed, I felt gravity pull away all the day's heavy burden. The weight disappeared, and my soul settled in this quiet place.

- "Everything is fine," written in my heart. I am safe in this space, shrouded in grace. I know that I am protected here, and my desire is always the same. There is nothing I need to fear now.

- Anything that feels bad inside can breathe. There is nothing that is not worth the cure for sleep. Compassionate people know what I have experienced. I am accepted. All worries have been relieved. Now I can also rest.

- When I settled down on the bed, my whole body was sighing. My breath rolled around like a tide. It's a relief to come here alive. This still moment is a gift—a waveless ocean, a breezy sky.

- I let go of all worries that I should not be here. There are no wrong decisions, no paths I don't intend to take. I swim purely and accept every message. It is the correct way.

- Fortunately, my idea is not me. I transcend all spiritual activities because I am of real consciousness. I allow ideas to enter and leave me easily; I let them be taken away like leaves in the breeze. I lie down and allow it because I am.

Affirmation for Relive Anxiety

"I find that using my voice to say the affirmation of anxiety is very effective in reducing anxiety symptoms." Sometimes, anxiety is caused by stress, but it feels like nothing for people with anxiety disorders. It ranges from general nervousness to feeling like a heart attack. Sometimes, anxiety attacks can be debilitating. The key to relieving anxiety attacks is to find a way to ground yourself. Talking to yourself or repeating words or phrases is a handy tool during anxiety attacks. "Positive affirmation of anxiety can help reduce fear and replace fear with more positive thoughts."

I find that using my voice to say affirmation of anxiety is very effective in reducing anxiety symptoms. Fortunately, I found a complimentary thinking app called Think Up that can help me relax in stressful situations by listening to the self-affirmations I recorded using the app. It brings me back to the present and inner wisdom. The soothing background music also calmed me down. It helped me focus on the affirmation of anxiety, thus eliminating all thoughts of racing.

My Feelings and Thoughts Are Correct

You have the right to enjoy your feelings, and expressing your emotions is very healthy. Anxiety is accompanied by genuine symptoms, which are not "all in your mind." Confirm your thoughts so that you can better understand your fears. Write it down or contact someone you trust. Also, if you feel that self-care is not enough, please remember to talk with your doctor!

Today, I First Take Care of My Body, Mind, And Soul

Sometimes, we all want to take a step back and show ourselves some TLC. Everyone's self-care looks different. It can be writing, eating many fruits and vegetables, or just enjoying a coffee in peace!

I will talk to myself, just like I am talking to my relatives. We were inspired by one of my favorite quotes! We should always talk to ourselves as if we were talking to our closest friends. When I inhale and then exhale slowly and steadily, I release the pressure. When you are struggling with anxiety, breathing exercises can be beneficial. Consider reading different methods and try to incorporate them into your daily work to help relieve stress.

I Am Loved

Anxiety often makes you feel unpleasant, but this is not the case. Some people care about you and want to see you happy and support your goals. Even though I have had a hard time so far, I can yet make the most of it. A few days ago, I secured myself out of the door, accidentally put a transparent shirt on a polka-dot bra, and sprinkled tea everywhere at Starbucks. Later that day, I still had a good time and laughed a lot. I don't have to justify myself to anyone because I am enough. Anxiety can make you sense that you are not good enough, but it is true. And you don't require to prove yourself to anyone because you are fantastic! Everyone's path is lovely, including my own. It is important to remember this, especially when you scroll through Instagram. Comparing games is enough to make you feel frustrated.

Tomorrow Is A Brand-New Day

No matter what you are experiencing now, things will get better. Today may not be the best, but tomorrow is a brand-new chapter. I had a difficult weekend, and Alejandro reminded me of this on Saturday.

I Am Safe; There Is No Threat from The World

This simple statement has a calming effect and can dispel the myth that people tell themselves under stressful situations. People usually convince themselves that they are in danger—whether emotionally, physically, or mentally. This feeling promotes an evolutionary stress response. To conquer this type of process, remind yourself that you are indeed safe and not threatened.

I Choose to Always Respond Positively to All Situations

When faced with stress, you are free to choose the best way to cope. In this case, remind yourself that a positive attitude is one thing you can control. Respond actively to help resolve this issue consciously and firmly.

My Experience Cannot Prevent My Future Success

In most cases, anxiety is a conditioned response to a specific disease. In most cases, anxiety is escalated or driven by the experience. If you decide to let anxiety control you, your experience will always hold you. However, if you realize that there are other ways, you can break the past and start over. When you forget history and focus on the infinite possibilities of today and tomorrow, changing your mindset can increase creativity.

Replace Unhealthy and Negative Thoughts

Anxiety affirmation—replace harmful and negative thoughts. To achieve positive success, you must know how to control your thoughts. It is a basic course because as long as you manage your thoughts, you can immediately stop all negative thoughts. Don't let wrong thoughts and fears stay in your mind; you should correct this situation by sorting your thoughts. However, this is not easy to achieve without a firm decision.

Is It Good or Bad?

It doesn't make sense to mark the situation as good or bad, because it is not. Each case has its lessons, and even if certain things seem negative, they may still contribute to your positive results in the future. It's hard to imagine this possibility, but, recognizing that you can still benefit from bad situations can alleviate your anxiety.

When I Relax and Breathe Slowly, Anxiety Will Radiate

The body and mind are closely connected. Therefore, getting your body out of tension can also help eliminate psychological stress. The relaxation of body muscles combined with deep and slow breathing reduces the body's pressure, thus creating an ideal environment for relaxation. Life is beautiful; I believe the world can help me live a remarkable experience.

- I've had enough.

- Every air I exhale, tension.

- Every day I feel more relaxed and calmer.

- I will make a significant contribution to my work

- Just like before, I will survive.

- When I breathe, my muscles relax.

- The stress disappeared from my mind and body.

- I am OK.

- I am strong. I'm ready for change.

- I know this situation is challenging to solve, but I am determined to go beyond it.

- You understood it!

- With my talent, I can provide more.

- I can breathe slowly anytime.

- By developing patience, I can get rid of anxiety.

- If I keep courage, I will overcome this situation.

- Always pay attention to details, I will ever win.

- I will complete one step at a time to be successful.

- I can do it now because life wants the best for me.

- I am currently in touch with the environment and feel comfortable.

- I like my life; I control it.

- I can prevent this.

- I will succeed.

- I can do anything.

- I celebrate the victory every day, no matter how big or small.

- Despite my fears, I will still live a real-life and follow my dreams.
- I let go of toxic and negative thoughts.
- I feel rooted at this moment.
- I can control my body.
- Today, I only choose happiness and joy.
- I accept changes and new opportunities.
- I hold my mind; it will never hold me.
- Now my life is full of fun.
- I can only accept healthy things into my life.
- I am a strong and independent person.
- The panic I feel is only temporary.
- I will smile, breathe, and walk slowly. During times of high stress, it may be challenging to slow down.
- I am giving my best and will continue to grow.
- I am a beautiful person inside out.
- I believe in myself.

- I can say no for my mental health

- It is easy to focus on the to-do list, but we should celebrate our growth, talents, and strengths. If you haven't heard of it today, that's great!

- Everything will be fine.

- I feel centered and rooted.

- I allow myself to receive supplies for Mental Health Day.

- As time passes by, I will continue to recover from past sufferings.

- I want to concentrate today-one hour at a time, one thing.

- Self-care is essential because I should be happy and satisfied.

- I am healthy and will spend the gloomiest days.

- I am unique, and I am loved. I am important.

- I am important, so I deserve.

- I can do it.

- I can freely follow the beauties around me.

- I have perseverance and a strong ability.

- I can use my inner strength to overcome anxiety.

- I can stop this.

- I will achieve it.

- I am calm. I am very relaxed.

- I got rid of my anxiety.

- I will overcome any stressful situation.

First, you should immediately bring any negative emotions into your mind. Instead of thinking, "If I go to the party alone, I will appear stupid," it is better to correct yourself quickly. Such thoughts are incorrect or useless in any respect and will only interfere with your thinking. Make wise decisions and move forward actively.

Keep reminding yourself that others will come and you will still be there. Tell yourself that you will have an unforgettable experience, and most of your friends will participate. These ideas will play a key role in shaping your way of thinking.

Controlling your thoughts is essential for active thinking and making informed decisions. Therefore, whenever an unhealthy and stupid idea comes up, consider the countless positive factors from the same situation. Cheer up and decide to move on!

- At this time, I choose to free the past and look forward to the beauty that awaits me.

- With every new breath, I inhale and exhale my fear. I learned that recovery and growth are safe for me.

- At this time, I choose to feel relaxed and peaceful. Everything is unfolding logically.

- I choose to fill my mind with positive, nurturing, and healing thoughts.

- There are no mistakes, only lessons. I have already done my best.

- My breathing is relaxed, and my breathing is tense.

- I am capable of solving any problems I face.

- I have no anxiety and lead a peaceful life.

- I eliminated negative thoughts and filled with positive reviews.

- Anxiety may make me uncomfortable, but I am responsible for my mind and body.

- Every moment I take a deep breath, I get calmer and calmer.

- I am drawing positive energy into my body.

- I didn't have anything that frustrated me.

- I have everything I need for a happy life.

- I can overcome anxiety.

- I am safe and controllable.

- The feeling of panic is leaving my body.

- My mind is clear, and I am in control.

- I free myself from stress.

- I am relaxing in every part of my body.

- I eliminated negative thoughts and filled with positive reviews.

- Every time I take a deep breath, I get calmer and calmer.

- I am in control now.

- My body is very calm.

- Everything is okay in my world.

- I didn't have anything that frustrated me. Although anxiety may make you feel that the world is bearing a heavy burden, it is not. Speaking positively to yourself can remind yourself that sometimes things don't always look like they are. It enables you to see things in a different light.

- Every time I breathe, I release my anxiety. Remember, it must be a positive idea. To get rid of stress, you must express positive thoughts about their disappearance. Therefore, tell yourself that every breath is a way to relieve anxiety. It is to provide a way out for anxiety and get rid of these feelings.

- I am healthy and can handle anything. Anxiety may make you feel incompetent, but remember that you are taking back the effects that stress seems to have on you when you use positive confirmation. You are speaking to your inner self and encouraging yourself. It's time to brag and say: "I already know!"

- I control my thoughts; they do not control me. Everyone encounters some anxious thoughts from time to time. When these thoughts become overwhelming and affect your mood, this is anxiety. You can admit these ideas. However, to overcome anxiety, acknowledging these ideas means keeping the point of view correct. You may feel anxious, but fear cannot control you.

- Who I am and what I do are significant? Even in the days when we feel inefficient in doing our best, what you do is essential. You are very important. You are important to others. Anxiety has a way to make people feel inferior. It may also make you think that any task you are trying to accomplish is stupid or not good enough. Don't let anxiety speak to your life. You talk about your life.

- I choose peace! In anxiety, it is easy to feel that there is no peace. Anxiety usually makes people feel confused. Speak to the inner self and choose peace. Tell yourself every day, "I choose peace."

- I am a winner—people who feel anxious to feel hopeless. Uncontrolled anxiety can lead to a sense of impending doom. When you start to handle this situation, please object to it. Tell yourself that you are a winner. Even if you seem to feel the opposite, please speak up.

- My challenge is my opportunity! We all face challenges. Part of becoming an overcomer is learning how to meet these challenges. Look at your challenges and don't think of them as obstacles, but as opportunities. Every time you face a challenge, you will become stronger. These challenges become stepping stones to great opportunities!

Affirmation to Help You Find Happiness

Happiness depends on our attitude towards life. Two different people may feel differently in the same situation, depending on their perspectives. For example, after completing an incredibly tricky task, a person may feel relieved that the "work" has been completed. Another person may be happy that he has completed the job, and one rest assured, one comfortable! Not everyone is born with a cheerful personality. But psychologists say that we can be trained to be happy. All that is needed is a small change in thinking. Happiness will help you change your mind. People are as excited as they make up their minds. "Experts say that we can do something regularly to bring happiness into our lives. Performing random acts of kindness are one of them. Another person who influences or is positively affecting your life is a way; regularly, creating a better future for yourself is another way.

For all of us, feeling happy is usually essential. Most of us pursue happiness in everything we do. We believe that when we achieve our goals, we will ultimately be satisfied. It is easier and more effective to focus solely on creating happy feelings now than waiting for something to inspire our ability to be satisfied. When we choose happy thoughts and set our intentions for a happy life, we are ready to achieve success and satisfaction in all aspects of life. Our sense of happiness will reflect on us a life full of opportunities and make you feel happier, and the more we focus, the more it will expand.

The Universe Is Good for Me

When you feel uncomfortable, it is hard to believe that the universe will support you and stand by your side. But this is what you require to do. Always remember that the universe is in your favor. Believe it, and repeat it once a day until it becomes a part of you because that is the only truth. The universe has been working hard to bring you joy, happiness, and all the positive things you deserve. All your dreams will become a reality one day—you have to believe it.

I Have Enough

You are enough, and you deserve it. There is no need to worry that it is only enough to achieve specific achievements in life. Things do not define you. You have enough to meet your needs, and you need to believe in it honestly.

I Should Be Healthy, Happy, And Successful

If you think you should be healthy, happy, and prosperous, then you will. However, it will be difficult for the universe to understand your message if you do not do this. It would help if you believed that you are worthy of the great things in life because by doing so, you will transmit positive vibrations to the universe. The universe will reward you with greater positivity. All of this is to establish a positive foundation to attract more positive emotions to your life.

My Heart Is Always Willing to Accept and Accept All Forms of Love

To obtain rich Happiness and blessings, you also need to be prepared to give. Your heart needs to be open, sharing, and receiving love in various forms. You need to live out love. Life with an open mind and an open mind is the first step in attracting more love and more positive things. It is essential to find a balance. It will be the cornerstone of future success and Happiness.

I Am Grateful for Everything I Have

When giving a positive affirmation of success and happiness, expressing gratitude for everything you already have is one of the most important things, because gratitude itself is a positive form. Therefore, instead of focusing on the things you don't have and want to have, you should focus on being grateful for the things you already have. It will put you in a higher positive state, which is the core of prosperity happiness.

Happiness is my birthright; I deserve to have all the good things in life. It would help if you believed that happiness is your birthright, not an impossible thing. You should feel happy, and you should have all the good things in life! You don't have to rise mountains to prove to yourself and others worthy of respect, love, and appreciation. You already have all of them. You need to find it and embrace it!

My Life Is Full of Happiness, Calm, Blessings, And Love

If you already understand that your life is full of happiness, peace, blessing, and love, you will live such a life. Remember, everything comes from your thoughts and ideas. You are, you become your idea. Therefore, please feel free to think and believe that your life is full of the biggest things in the world, and the universe will work harder with your support.

I Strive to Be A Better Self

Always focus on improving your habits and put your energy into being better, bigger, and healthier. It would support if you worked hard to be a better version of yourself because this is the only way for all the good things in life to be rewarded. The universe needs to know that you are doing your best to realize your potential.

I Will Choose Happiness Anyway

It is my favorite and one of the most complicated. When life disappoints you, it is challenging to choose to stay happy anyway, but it is necessary. Why? Because the primary purpose of every challenge and every hardship is to make you stronger, more resilient, and wiser. When something unfortunate happens, it is better to choose to get rid of the difficulties than to live in pain.

Happiness Makes Me Excited

Believe that happiness is the only medicine for your soul and the only powerful force that can lift your spirits. Live happiness, imagine happiness, and get excited about all the little things that matter. The essence of true happiness is existing every day as if this is your last day because it will be so one day. "My natural position is the abundance of joy and unconditional love."

When you believe that your real state is made up of happiness and unconditional love, you will begin this kind of life, and you will start to attract more positive things to your life. Everything is to express gratitude for what you have, believe that you deserve to be great, and act as if you already have it. That is the only secret to attract a lot of Happiness and success in daily life.

I Trust My Instinct

The intuition is that only a small voice in your head can tell you when you are wrong or when you are right. When making a decision, you need to believe in this voice, and you require to believe that it will support you in making wise decisions and protect you from all negative factors in your life. "I am surrounded by positive people who believe in me wholeheartedly."

The most significant source of negative emotions is that everyone around you is planning something that is not good for you or is jealous of your success. It would help if you were with positive people who believe in you wholeheartedly and be happy with your success. Moreover, it would help if you keep reminding yourself, because the more you think about it, the more positive people the universe will bring into your life, and they will be your most significant support.

I Am Passionate, Creative, And Determined to Do Anything

The key to success includes the following three words: passion, creativity, and determination. Passion will make your life full of love. Creativity will ensure that you will never get bored, and determination will give you the strength to move on, even if you think you will not. If you practice this affirmative attitude several times a day, your work, hobbies, and everything you do will be greatly improved. You will get considerable achievements and be rewarded accordingly.

- "Every day, I become happier in various ways."

- "Happiness is my birthright. I choose Happiness; I should be happy."

- "Happiness is contagious. I spread Happiness to others and absorb the Happiness of others."

- "I moved many lives. My Happiness does all these people happy, thus making it a big happy world."

- "My happy character makes happiness into my life. I only interact with happy people, only happy experiences."

- "The whole process of life makes me happy. Moving towards my goal makes me happy."

- "I thank God for a good life. I thank everyone who moved my life and made it worth living."

- "I like every moment of the day."

- "Happiness is my motto."

- "Happiness is easy for me."

- "Happiness is my second instinct."

- "I regularly perform random acts of kindness. Kindness breeds love, and love brings happiness."

- "I am very grateful; miracles, happiness, and joy attract me."

- "I am very grateful for guidance and excitement. Now, everything I need to be happy flows through me."

- "I allow myself to grow, and the energy of happiness passes through me now."

- "I decide to be happy and grateful today."

- "I now have everything I need to be happy."

- "My heart is always open, radiating love, and joy."

- "Life is getting better and better every day."

- "Today, I let the energy of happiness flow through me, filling me with joy."

- "I am good; I am glad; I am strong."

- "I am easily creating a happy life I want."

- "I am happy to accept happiness, light, and love."

- "I chose to watch this with love, and I let the universe do her thing."

- "In this case, I would like to see the benefits. Now life is working hard for me."

- "Love is everywhere; I am worthy of love."

- "I am beautiful, bold, and brave."

- "I am surrounded by love, and it's good."

- "Today, I am willing to find good things for my life."

- "Life supports me, and new doors are always opening for me."

- "Today is full of miracles!"

- "Every day makes me feel happier and happier in various ways."

- "Today, I choose to be happy; I deserve to be happy."

- "Everything is going perfectly."

- "I started to notice how happy and positive I was."

- "I choose to feel happy, no matter where I go, positive energy will follow me."

- "Life is working for me, and I start to feel happier; how can I be better than this."

- "I am building the life I want with my good feelings."

- "I get the support of life, and I let go and make myself happy."

- "I am willing to accept myself unconditionally."

- "I allow myself to let go now and be happy."

- "I have all the happiness, love, and positive energy I need for the happiest day."

- "Today, I let myself feel the beauty around me and stay happy and positive throughout the day."

- "I attract more and more love, joy, and happiness in my life every day."

- "Today, I am grateful for my happiness and positive energy."

- "My natural state is love, and I should be happy."

- "My life is full of happiness, peace, and love."

- "I am peaceful, happy, healthy, and have the freedom to be me."

- "I am surrounded by peace, harmony, and vitality."

- "I should feel happy and satisfied."

- "All the good life I deserve."

- "I accept the beauty that flows in life."

- "I attract health, wealth, happiness, and love effortlessly."

- "I focus on enjoying life and find happiness in every place I see."

- "I allow myself to feel happy and satisfied."

- "No matter where I go, I can attract happiness and joy."

- "No trouble where I go, I am willing to accept love, friendliness, and happiness."

- "It's time to shine! I'm ready to exit the life of my dreams."

- "Happiness is my birthright. All the good life I deserve is worthy of now and accepting."

- "I can shape the ideal reality."

- "I create the life I want with good emotions."

- "Everything is always nice to me."

- "When I feel happy, I will show more reasons to be happy."

- "I am willing to be happy now."

- "I accept that Happiness is my nature."

- "I deserve to be happy."

- "My Happiness comes from my heart."

- "I create Happiness by accepting every part of myself through unconditional love."

- "Happiness is the essence of my existence."

- "I have seen many positive aspects of my life."

- "I keep creating everything I desire in my heart."

- "I feel happy in everything I do."

- "I am convinced of myself as a person."

- "I allow myself to be happy."

- "I make myself feel good."

- "Happiness creates the life I have always dreamed of I choose now."

- "The joy of following me reveals the path to the best life."

- "I choose. Happiness will keep me in perfect health. "

- "Everyone around me feels Happiness."

- "I use Happiness to create the possibility of happiness for others."

- "I am destined to live a happy life."

- "When sharing with others, my inner Happiness expands."

- "All the good things in my life result from my willingness to find Happiness at every moment."

- "My Happiness is reflected in me in everything I attract."

- "My inner Happiness is the source of all the good in my life."

- "I feel happy in everything I do."

Chapter 6. What is Hypnosis

Hypnosis is a mental state similar to sleep. In this state, you are very susceptible to hints or guidance from a hypnotist. During the hypnosis process, you will enter a more focused and attentive state. A hypnotist can help you relax and become calm, which makes you more open to suggestions. Hypnosis is equivalent to daydreaming. When you are daydreaming, you tend to obscure other thoughts or stimuli and focus only on your daydreams. During the hypnosis process, you also tend to concentrate fully on what is happening at the moment without being misled by other thoughts or sounds.

Hypnosis can be used to treat various diseases, conditions, and discomforts. For example, suggestiveness caused by hypnosis can relieve anxiety or depression. Hypnosis can also be applied to treat certain medical disorders, such as gastrointestinal diseases, skin diseases, or chronic pain. However, hypnosis is not suitable for all situations. Researchers also use hypnosis to obtain information about its effects on learning, memory, sensation, and perception.

To better understand how hypnosis works, let's look at an example. Imagine you bite your nails and want to get rid of this bad habit. For this, please schedule a meeting with a hypnotist.

When you enter the room, the hypnotist will ask you to choose a place to sit or lie down. You sit in a chair, and the hypnotist asks what you want to do. You tell him that you want to stop biting your nails, so the hypnotist asks you to close your eyes and imagine that you are in a place you like, such as a beach or a park. The hypnotist will guide you through some visualization operations to make you feel calm and relaxed.

After relaxing, the hypnotist suggests that you no longer need to bite your nails. He asks you to visualize healthy and well-manicured nails. In your extremely calm state, this suggestion may have a more significant impact on your thinking than in other situations. Your healthy, quiet, and relaxed mood makes you very suggestive. After generating the suggested mental image, the hypnotist will use the phrase "Now it's time to go back to the present" to trick you into opening your eyes; this way, the conversation ends.

For more than 200 years, people have been thinking and arguing about hypnosis. Still, science has not yet fully explained how hypnosis occurs. We see what a character does under hypnosis, but we don't know why they do it. This problem is a small part of a larger problem: how the human mind works. In the foreseeable future, scientists are unlikely to give an exact explanation of the reason, so useful hypnotism will remain a mystery.

Hypnosis for Deep Sleep

But psychiatrists do know the general properties of hypnosis, and they have some understanding of how hypnosis works. It is an extreme state, with a strong suggestion, relaxation, and enhanced imagination. It is not really like sleeping, because the subject is always alert. It is often analyzed to daydreaming or the feeling of "losing yourself." You are fully conscious but can mediate most of the stimuli around you. You focus on the subject at hand and almost exclude any other ideas.

In the daily state of daydreams or movies, a fictional world seems a little real to you because it can fully stimulate your emotions. The imaginary event can cause real fear, sadness, or happiness. If you are surprised at something (for example, a monster jumping from the shadows), you may even sit on the seat and shake. Some researchers classify all these actions as forms of self-hypnosis. The leading hypnosis expert in the 20th century believed that people were hypnotized every day. But most psychiatrists focus on the state brought about by deliberate relaxation and concentrated exercise. This deep hypnosis is usually compared to the relaxed mental state between wakefulness and sleep.

In traditional hypnosis, you will approach the hypnotist's suggestions or your ideas as if they were realistic. If the hypnotist recommends that your tongue is twice as large, you will feel discomfort in your mouth, and you may have trouble speaking. If the hypnotist suggests drinking a chocolate milkshake, you will taste the milkshake and feel that it cools your mouth and throat. If the hypnotist advises you to be afraid, you may panic or start to sweat. But all along, you know this is all fiction. In essence, like a child, you are violently "pretending."

In this unique psychological state, people will feel at ease and relaxed. Presumably, this is because they have eliminated the worries and doubts that would generally prevent their actions. When watching a movie, you may experience the same feeling: when you are fully absorbed in the plot, worries about work, family, etc. gradually disappear until all you think about is everything that appears on the screen.

In this state, you are also very likely to be inspired. In other words, when the hypnotist tells you to do something, you may fully accept the idea. It is what makes stage hypnotists so interesting. Under normal circumstances, sane adults suddenly walk around the stage, giggling like a chicken, or singing on top of their lungs. The fear of embarrassment seemed to fly out the window. However, throughout the experience, the subjects' sense of security and morality are still deeply rooted.

Hypnosis and Sleep

A persistent misconception about hypnotism is that it is sleeping. It's easy to see how this came about. People in a deep hypnotic state certainly look like they are sleeping, with the same changes in breathing style, facial color, and muscle tension. Many hypnotists still use the "sleep" command when inducing ancestry. Indeed, the word hypnosis appears from the Greek "Hypnos," which means sleep. However, hypnosis is not sleeping, although it has some essential characteristics.

Psychologists' research on dreams' role and function gave us a breakthrough in the relationship between hypnosis and sleep. Since all mammals are dreaming, dreaming is likely to serve a primary evolutionary purpose (rather than a rare psychological purpose), unless you think that a cat or dog needs psychological analysis. In short, the dream is realized in a strangely symbolic way, which happened the day before. More importantly, their actions aroused our emotions in some way. Emotional arousal is inevitable in the daytime; countless things happen to us, whether positive or negative, which will activate our instinct. Suppose someone cut a person in front of you while driving, which made you angry, or the boss told you something that made you unhappy.

If we express these emotions in a certain way, they will be released and completed. You may verbally express your opinions about other people's driving, but you may not represent your feelings to your boss. However, your emotions have been aroused, and when you sleep at night, they are still produced. It is almost certain that you will make your dream come true and express your feelings in a weird metaphorical way—maybe you will find yourself yelling at monsters, French presidents, or other things that symbolize your boss.

The reason for this is to rush out of unresolved emotions so that we wake up refreshed, our nervous system is intact, stress-free, and ready to meet the needs of the next day. If we don't, if we keep with us unresolved emotions, we will soon be in big trouble. Our nervous system will be overloaded.

So, what does this have to do with hypnosis? The key is rapid eye movement or REM state. It looks like a computer interface and serves two purposes. First of all, this is the first way that nature uses our instinctive behavior to program us—before we are born, we all experience a lot of REM in the womb. It ensures that every baby is born with the basic instincts needed to survive outside, such as the instinct to breastfeed.

Second, REM is a means to keep the original instinct programming up-to-date and in good condition. It is crucial in evolutionary terms if your intuition is weak or outdated, and the long-term prospects will not be desirable! Therefore, we need the ability to learn from experience, and the ability to eliminate stress from the instinctive nervous system—REM performs these two tasks.

The REM state is most often associated with the sleep required for dream sleep and can be regarded as a maintenance task; however, It can also be activated, when we daydream, when we vividly recall things in our memory. When we experience any form of hypnotic trance, it is also there. Indeed, hypnosis is nothing more than deliberately creating rapid eye movements in ourselves and others.

It explains why people in a deep hypnotic state sometimes act as if they are dreaming in a dream. It is because, even if they are not sleeping, they are the same as what happened when they were asleep. For example, the hypnotized object often hallucinates non-existent things, such as stage hypnosis, vividly displayed. When you consider that every time we sleep and dream, we have hallucinations, which is not strange.

If hypnosis is another way to create a REM state, then it also performs the same update and maintenance tasks as REM. Just being in a REM/hypnotic state is enough to allow the overloaded brain to catch up with its housekeeping and shut down unresolved emotional arousal. It is why people often say that they feel better after hypnosis and can think more clearly. By deliberately activating the REM state, hypnosis can also open up the interface with the unconscious. In this way, new behavior patterns can be determined on the subconscious level of instinctive behavior, to play the most significant role in the best model.

Sleep Hypnosis Science

James Braid was a surgeon, scientist, and pioneer of modern hypnotism in the 19th century. He hypnotized patients to assist in surgery. The Braid is designed to relieve pain and slow bleeding, and surprisingly, his patients have a higher survival rate.

Since it is easy to record Braid's post-operative success as a placebo effect, it would help understand the latest research on the impact of hypnosis on sleep. Is it effective? The contemporary science is in favor of an overwhelming majority.

The exciting news for light sleepers is that a 2014 study found that hypnosis can increase slow-wave sleep (deep sleep) in some sleepers by 80%. "The results may be critical for patients and elderly people with sleep problems." Parents of children with insufficient sleep can also breathe a sigh of relief. Another study reviewed hypnosis as a treatment for sleep problems in school-age children. The report concluded that hypnosis is an effective way to treat insomnia in children under seven years.

The adverse side effects of sleep aids are usually worrying. Still, a recent study shows that sleep hypnosis is unlikely to have adverse effects. A review of 139 studies on hypnosis's products to improve sleep found that most studies showed positive results and no side effects. The researchers concluded: "Hypnotherapy for sleep problems seems to be a promising treatment, with almost no evidence of adverse events."

These studies are just evidence that hypnosis is a natural way to get deep, nourishing sleep. To start a sleep hypnosis experiment safely and effectively, you recommend that you try the Relax Melodies app for hypnosis. They are narrated in a soothing voice and are designed to guide you into a deep and peaceful sleep.

What Is Sleep Hypnosis?

Sleep hypnosis involves listening to a hypnotherapist's verbal cues to bring you into a state with the suggested force. Hypnotherapists use different methods to induce relaxation, such as concentration, symptom control, and guided imaging. People who are hypnotized may hear phrases such as "relax," "deep," "relaxed," and "let go." These words are meant to encourage someone to drift into sleep.

Hypnosis is a mental state similar to sleep. In this state, the brain is entirely relaxed and accepts specific external suggestions. It usually requires trained professionals to achieve this status safely and successfully.

Sleep hypnosis is used to help people fall asleep, stay asleep, and get better sleep. The person listens to prompts, which may cause deep relaxation and induce a state of comfortable falling asleep. Sleep hypnosis can be performed with a hypnotherapist or through recording. When you focus on what you are saying and nothing else, it may be repeated words. It can be soft music with instructive visual suggestions that can put you in an ideal environment for relaxation and deep sleep. Contrary to some ancient beliefs, you can control your body and mind. Sleep hypnosis courses include:

Settle Down: The recipient lies down and feels comfortable.

Let Go: Lead the audience to put aside all doubts or worries.

Induction: By releasing conscious thinking and opening up the subconscious, the listener can relax more deeply.

Breathing: This part includes conscious breathing to make the recipient more relaxed.

Suggestion: The longest and final part of hypnosis includes guiding images and implanting the desired results into the listener's subconscious.

You may be wondering whether hypnosis is wishful thinking or feasible. Fortunately, there is a lot of research on sleep hypnosis.

Does It Work?

Hypnotherapy may be more effective for some people than others, depending on their level of "recommendation," which means they are eager to believe that this approach will be useful.

However, research shows that about a quarter of people cannot be hypnotized at all. Other studies have found that to obtain any benefit, it may be necessary to combine sleep hypnosis with Cognitive-Behavioral Therapy. Therefore, as an independent treatment for sleep problems, hypnotism may not be the most successful option.

If done correctly, sleep hypnosis is a safe and effective way to get rid of sleep. It is recommended that one needs to be open and believe in the concept of sleep hypnosis to make it useful. Despite this, about 25% of people cannot be hypnotized. These people will not be affected by the advice at all. If you belong to this type of person, sleep hypnosis will not work for you. The only way to find out if you can be hypnotized is to try it.

Evidence of Self-Hypnosis during Sleep

We have seen that hypnotherapists have different opinions on whether hypnosis during sleep is useful. But what does the evidence say?

1998 Study on Subconscious Learning during Sleep

Research on the brain has been progressing. Although this research was conducted more than 20 years ago and made significant progress since then, it is still closely related to today. In fact, since most views on hypnotherapy are the same as those 50 years ago, we can consider the conclusions presented in this study to be the most recent. This research was considered a breakthrough at the time because it used specific medical equipment (CT scans and MRI) that we still use in hospitals today.

This research was conducted at the famous Johns Hopkins University. The electrodes of the subjects participating in the study were directly implanted in the brain, specifically in the cerebral cortex. With the help of electrodes, scientists can pinpoint the brain area responsible for our hearing. But this study went even further and explored what happens if subjects listen to various audios during waking, light sleep cycles, and deep sleep.

The exciting thing about this study is that it proves that our brain is aware of acoustics during sleep. Now, this study does not test whether subjects can recall any sounds they heard during sleep, but because of this study, we can be sure that the brain makes noise during sleep.

2012 Research on Subconscious Learning during Sleep

In 2012, scientists at Northwestern University published a fascinating study. According to this research, if you practice specific music, listening to music again while you sleep can help you play the music more accurately when you wake up. Participants in this study learned to press the keys in sequence to play two songs, which is similar to what you see in popular video games such as "Guitar Hero." During the nap, when the subject's brain was affected by slow-wave sleep, one of the tunes was played repeatedly. Slow-wave rest is considered a critical period for memory consolidation.

When the participants woke up, their two tones improved, indicating that the nap helped them consolidate their newly discovered knowledge. However, the accuracy of the sounds (not known) heard by the subjects during sleep was much improved. The conclusion of this study shows that our brain can not only listen to what is happening during sleep but also remember what we hear.

2015 Research on Subconscious Learning during Sleep

Scientists conducted a new study on subconscious learning during sleep in 2015. This focuses on how the brain works during sleep when hearing sounds. Scientists use electroencephalogram (EEG) machines to record brain activity. The EEG machine uses tiny sensors attached to the subject's scalp to pick up electrical signals generated by the brain to support cells' communication. EEG machines are used in brain scans in hospitals around the world.

As you can see in the picture above, I also keep an EEG machine. I use this device to explain my hypnotherapy clients in real-time how their brains work. Although expensive, my equipment is far less complicated than the equipment used in the world's top hospitals.

Studies have shown that the brain does not shut down during sleep. Instead of hitting do, the mind is busy checking and storing memories. But the brain is more active during sleep than previously thought. According to this research, the brain processes auditory information as if it were awake. Not only that, but the brain responds to meaningful information first. More importantly, even if we are fast asleep, the brain will interact with language information.

It is the latest study using modern technology to study the brain, so we can consider adopting the latest technology. The study concluded that the brain could not only hear information; it can also process data and prepare to respond and make decisions while we sleep. Therefore, we can safely say that the brain is active and can learn while sleeping.

Is Sleeping Effectively During Hypnosis?

The views of hypnotists are divided. Some of them believe that hypnosis is effective when sleeping, while some do not. However, scientific research shows that there is clear evidence that falling asleep during hypnosis is still effective. I believe I will return to this blog post and update it as time passes, and new information is released. For now, we can securely say that even if some hypnotists may disagree, falling asleep during hypnosis is an effective way to solve your problems. Views may be outdated or based on false beliefs, but scientific research is always an indicator that we can trust.

What Is Meditation Sleep?

Meditation trains us to reduce brainstorming and learn more about the current moment. When we suddenly stop and remain still, the tendency to fall into thoughts may be most vital. Sleep meditation is a unique guided experience that alone provides natural sleep assistance, allowing us to let go of everything that happens, and everything said to relax while relaxing. In scientific terms, meditation helps reduce the heart rate by igniting the parasympathetic nervous system and encouraging slow breathing, thereby increasing night sleep quality. During sleep-based meditation, you may discover new tools and techniques to help relax your mind and body, allowing you to relax and unwind.

What Makes People Get Up at Night?

Almost half of us are deprived of sleep – but not because we don't want to sleep. Sometimes, we cannot fall asleep or stay asleep due to multiple biological factors and lifestyle choices. You know what's going on: Put your head on the pillow, and it seems that the brain suddenly becomes speeding. Of course, this idea has always existed. Just without any interference, you will be aware of them.

Technology also exacerbates sleep problems: 90% of Americans use technology (including watching TV, using mobile phones, playing video games, using computers, etc.) within an hour before going to bed. Many of us even sleep with our phones lying under the pillows or beside our faces next to the ringers. Unfortunately, the use of blind screens and technology is negatively correlated with sound sleep: A study has shown that the more devices a person uses in a day, the more difficult it is for them to fall asleep and stay asleep. These effects mainly occur in people who use their devices highly throughout the day, even those who fall asleep with their phone ringing on (even as an alarm clock) or other nearby disruptive devices.

Benefits of Sleep Meditation

Sleeping shorter than seven hours a night increases the risk of heart disease, diabetes, and unhealthy eating habits, leading to other chronic diseases. Lack of sleep can lead to impaired short and long-term memory, decision-making, attention, and reaction time. People with insufficient sleep also tend to make more mistakes and drive more dangerously on the road. On the other hand, increasing sleep and improving sleep can reduce stress levels and improve mental clarity and memory. Upgrade sleep will also affect our immune system, encourage better eating habits and weight management.

Better sleep is even associated with reducing the risk of Alzheimer's. Research regularly associates improved sleep by providing better health. Why did you choose to meditate before going to bed? Especially if you have insomnia or difficulty when falling asleep, meditation can improve sleep quality and efficiency, how long you fall asleep, and how large you can stay awake during the day. Completing meditation before bed can help you fall asleep faster. Once you fall asleep, you may also sleep better.

Guided Sleep Meditation Techniques

Breathing exercise involves regulating breathing (for example, counting breaths) and eventually slowing the breathing slightly, which waves the body that it is time to sleep.

- **Pay Attention to Body Scans:** When you are lying in bed, you may be asked to pay attention to breathing and where your body touches the ground. Then, starting from the toes, you can consider gradually "turning off" any force in various parts of your body.

- **Visualization:** Visualization requires you to imagine an image or scene, and then brings you into a mental state similar to hypnosis.

- **Gratitude:** Some sleep-focused meditation programs focus on appreciation meditation and love meditation, which requires you to focus on gratitude.

- **Counting:** To slow down your thinking speed and get you out of cyclical thinking patterns, you may be invited to count slowly: count down from 10 (or even 1,000), and then start from 10.

- **Silence:** The narrator or guide may ask you to remain silent for a few minutes, up to a few minutes, with very little guidance. It is a way to concentrate after a long and busy day.

- **Exercise-Based Meditation:** If you are personally guided by sleep-based meditation, you may be invited to participate in mindfulness exercises such as Tai Chi, low-impact postures, or light stretching exercises.

- **Looking Back at Your Day:** Looking back at your day in detail and action by action may be an excellent way to distract. From waking up in the morning, getting a shower, and eating breakfast, spend 20 to 25 seconds a day, regardless of them.

Ten-Step Meditation Practice to Improve Sleep

It is no doubt that meditation can help us fall asleep better. Certain meditation practices can help us nod when we are overthinking. In the following exercises, headspace meditation experts share some insights to make your head feel more comfortable when you hit the pillow. Remember, this is not an exercise method to get you to sleep, but to raise your awareness and thoughts at night. It happens that it often causes sleep.

Step 1

After lying comfortably in bed, take five deep breaths, breath through your nose, and breathe through your mouth. When living, try to fill the lungs with air and expand the chest. As you breathe, imagine that your thoughts and feelings during the day disappear into the distance, while any tension in your body disappears. It will support the body and mind to prepare for future exercises.

Step 2

Start with the physical and mental occupancy state (how you feel). Remember, in the same way, and you can't rush to relax, you can't run to sleep, so please take some time to practice. Don't worry if many ideas are going around (this is normal). Now, let them do their own thing. Whatever you do, you should avoid the temptation to resist ideas, no matter how restless or uncomfortable they are.

Step 3

Next, learn more about physical contact points. Return your attention to your body's feeling touching the bed, and your body weight sinks into the mattress. Note that the most vital point of contact is the weight evenly distributed. You can also remark on any sounds or other feelings. The sound is especially disturbing when trying to fall asleep. First, it is helpful to know whether it is a sound that can be changed or a sound that cannot be controlled. Then, instead of obstructing the sound, place the sound gently on it, keep it in the sound for about 30 seconds, and turn your attention to the body.

Step 4

Now try to understand how the body feels. First, commonly do this. For example, does the body sense heavy or light, restless, or still? Then, scan the body down with the spirit from head to toe and gently observe any tension or tightness to obtain a more accurate image. The mind is always attracted to tension areas, but you can relax and know that you are going to sleep, and exercise will help release these areas. You can perform this scan multiple times, and each time it takes about 20 to 30 seconds.

Remember to pay attention to areas of relaxation and comfort and any areas of discomfort.

Step 5

By now, you may have noticed the rising and falling sensations of your breathing, but if you haven't seen yet, turn your attention to the position on your body where you can feel the movement the most. As always, please don't attempt to change the rhythm of breathing in any way, but let the body do its own thing. There is no right or wrong way of living in this exercise, so if you feel more chest than abdomen, don't worry. Note whether the breathing is deep or shallow, long or short, smooth or irregular.

Step 6

When you observe breathing for a minute or two, your mind will drift, which is normal. When you understand that you have been distracted, your mind drifts away. At that moment, you return to the present moment. All you have to do is to gently restore your attention to the feeling of rising and falling. You don't need to schedule this part of the exercise; as long as it feels like a few minutes have moved, you can move to the next part naturally.

Step 7

The next part of this exercise is about looking back at the past in a focused and structured way. Start from the first moment you can remember when you wake up in the morning. Do you remember how you felt when you woke up? Now, it's as if your brain has been set to a very gentle "fast forward"; watch your mind replay the day's events, meetings, and conversations. No need to elaborate; it's just an overview, a series of snapshots running through the mind.

Until now, the whole process took about three minutes. A few minutes seems appropriate, but as I said, this is just an overview of the day, so don't exceed three to four minutes. After a few days, you will no doubt be satisfied with its speed. As the thought repeats itself, the inevitable temptation will jump in and fall into thinking. First of all, it is normal for the mind to wander like this, but obviously, participating in a new review at this time of the night is not helpful. So, as before, when you realize that you are distracted, gently return to the movie playing and continue from where you left off.

Step 8

Cheer up, until now, and you can now return to your body. Please focus on the little toe of your left foot and imagine you turn it off at night. You can even repeat these words. When you focus on your toes, you will "close" or "rest" in your mind. It's as if you want muscles, joints, bones, and everything else to be allowed to turn off the power at night, knowing that you don't need to turn them on again until morning.

Step 9

Do the same for the next toe and the next toe, and so on. In this way, continue to pass through the ball of the foot, arch, heel, ankle, the lower part of the leg, all the way to the hip and pelvic area. Before repeating this exercise with your right leg, please take a moment to notice the difference in sensation between the "closed" portion and the one that is not "closed." If you doubt whether or not it happened while performing this exercise, you can feel it now. Repeat the same practice on the right leg, again starting from the toes and to the waist.

Step 10

Continue this exercise through the torso, arms, hands and fingers, throat, neck, face, and head upwards. Take time to enjoy the feeling of getting rid of tension without having to do anything with your body and giving up control. Now, you can let your thoughts wander as you want, no matter where you want to go, you can freely transfer from one idea to another until you fall asleep.

Why Should I Try to Fall Asleep?

Stress and Illness

Worrying about work, finances, family, and health can be very stressful, leading to anxiety and even illness. It is important to effectively manage stress levels so that they do not cause long-term health problems.

Bad Habits and Interruptions in Daily Work

It turns out that drinking caffeine or alcohol before going to bed can interfere with sleep. It is imperative to break bad habits and establish a healthy daily routine. Unpredictable days will prevent you from establishing a stable sleep pattern. Sleeping at a similar time every night and waking up at an equal time every morning can keep our body in a healthy sleep-wake cycle.

Travel and Jet Lag

If you are used to touring countries with different time zones, jet lag may be a common cause of difficulty falling asleep, staying asleep, or staying awake during the day. Jet lag is also related to loss of appetite and digestive problems.

Shift Work Barriers

Early morning work, night shift, or shift work plus difficulty falling asleep may mean that you have a shift work disorder.

People with this disease tend to feel sleep deprivation, which may impact overall health and well-being, such as depression, inattention, and insomnia.

Delayed Sleep Phase Disorder (DSPs)

If you need a few hours to fall asleep each night, you may be affected by DSPS. Since about 7% to 16% of people are diagnosed with DSPS, it is classified as a common disease.

An Advanced Sleep Disorder (ASPD)

ASPD is the opposite of "Delayed Sleep Stage Disorder." People with ASPD do not struggle to fall asleep at night but tend to fall asleep in the evening and wake up early. People who fight with ASPD are often referred to as "extremely early birds."

Narcolepsy

People with narcolepsy struggle with excessive sleepiness, sleep onset, and sleep paralysis during the day, and often fall asleep at inappropriate times. Narcolepsy is a long-term brain disease that is very rare because it is estimated to affect only 30,000 people in the UK.

Insomnia

Insomnia is a very usual sleep disorder, and people face great difficulty in falling asleep. It is estimated that in the UK, 1 in 3 people is affected. If you have insomnia, it is recommended that you seek more professional treatment.

Restless Legs Syndrome

If you have a great urge to exercise your legs when trying to fall asleep, you may have restless legs syndrome. If the situation is not too serious, some small adjustments to your daily activities can help you solve this problem.

Sleep Apnea

Beating at night, choking, gasping, or not breathing are all signs of sleep apnea. Although lifestyle changes can improve this situation, it is recommended that you seek medical help from a local family doctor or sleep specialist because of health risks.

Deep Sleep Meditation Techniques

Mindfulness Meditation

It is one of the most popular meditation methods during the day or night. Mindfulness requires you to pay close attention to your experience and environment. Although this technique sounds almost basic knowledge, putting it into practice can make a difference. For beginners, you can focus on breathing. "Our Mind works: Guided Meditation App" contains all the instructions you need. After you learn to turn your attention to your breath and distract your attention and pass by like a cloud in the sky (or sheep jumping over a door), you can try to practice other meditation objects, such as feelings. You can check your body, pay attention, and release tension; or sound, such as the patter of raindrops on the window glass.

Thanks to mindfulness meditation, you can become more aware of what is happening inside yourself and become more proficient. It can set aside restlessness and distraction without making yourself emotionally unstable. According to the famous meditation teacher, we have a gold mine inside. This gold mine is the ultimate cause of our tranquility and true happiness. By learning how to deal with irritability and distraction effectively, you will have ample opportunities to showcase and make the most of this gold mine.

Meditate

This meditation has some of the same characteristics as mindfulness because it requires little attention. However, here, we no longer focus on breathing but use positive affirmation to replace any disturbance that keeps us awake. Such as "My body is as peaceful as a mountain lake," "My mind is at ease," "I Breathe God, I call for peace, "Love is my nature; love is the essence of the universe," etc. Choose the affirmation that is meaningful to you. In addition to confirmation, you can also use the mantra of a particular faith tradition. Psychologists believe that when we fall asleep, our thoughts are deeply rooted in our subconscious minds. Positive affirmation can not only help us fall asleep but also can enhance the residual effect.

Guided Meditation Sleep

Sometimes, listening to the meditation teacher's voice is what you need to help you fall asleep. In guided sleep meditation, the instructor (usually in a soothing voice) guides you throughout the meditation process. They may require you to relax your toes, take a deep breath, or even your legs. They may also make you imagine a series of relaxing images. For example, the lecturer can invite you to imagine a beautiful beach and picture yourself sitting happily and peacefully along the water's edge. At the same time, the waves gently scratch your feet. Imagine the air you breathe and use distant seabirds to sing as your lullaby-see, you are already yawning, aren't you?

Tonight, leave anything that causes restlessness and distraction in another room, and then try to meditate. You can practice these methods after sitting in your seat or lying down in bed at night. No matter which style you choose, remember that besides helping sleep disorders, meditation has many other benefits that are recently discovered. Meditation can help you eliminate negative emotions and ways of thinking, giving you the insight to deal with trauma or grief and encourage recovery. Meditating hard can help cultivate compassion and be kind to others. What a healthy way of sleeping! Sweet dream!

Mantra Meditation

This technique involves repeating specific sounds to calm your body and calm the buzzing thoughts in your mind. Repetitive mantras are believed to help you eliminate distracting or stressful thoughts, allowing you to bring peace and tranquility to your mind. The term mantra has two parts: "man," which is derived from Sanskrit. Mantras are "tools of thought." It means "public voice." Of course, the most popular mantra is "Om" (or aum). Don't you feel the "hum"? No problem. Let you select which sound suits you best. Then repeat it until your views seem quieter, and you feel more peaceful (and sleepy).

Vipassana Meditation

In the Buddhist culture, the name "Vipassana" means "insight into the true nature of reality." Essentially, this form of meditation involves the use of self-observation to observe the real face of things. It means identifying the ideals and disadvantages of your true nature without judging yourself.

To try, consider what might be annoying activities that day. Ask yourself: Did that matter make me uncomfortable or sad? What actions should I take to reconcile this situation within myself? How can I get rid of this feeling to "stay today" and not carry it on to tomorrow? Or, how can I react so that it is not severely affected? Taking your thoughts seriously and honestly before going to bed may reduce stress and reduce sleep at later days. It will help both of you fall asleep and stay asleep all night so that you can bargain with stressful situations more effectively in the future.

Chapter 7. Visualize Your Path through Meditation

As a human being, one of the most inspiring and powerful things you can do is visualize what you want to express and then make it happen. The power of the mind is fantastic and coupled with mindfulness-based exercises such as meditation. You can enhance your ability to leapfrog development to create the life you want. Goal setting is the catalyst to achieve this goal. The aim of setting goals is to achieve the desired results. When intentions, actions, motivation, and focus are used carefully, setting, and achieving objectives can make your goals from now to now. But first, you must know where it is. "Where" starts with your vision.

The first step is to start with the ending and then go backward. The result is your highest vision for a particular area of life-health and fitness, relationships, family, occupation, or financial status. After establishing a connection with your vision, you need to set specific goals to help you achieve your dream. Many people think that the goal is the result and mistake the destination for the vision. They set a goal without considering in advance that the plan will make them a long-term or possessed goal. To make the most of the goal-setting process, it is important to link it to the quality of the lifestyle you ultimately want to live. To make the content clearer, let us outline the main difference between vision and goal.

Your Vision and Goals

Your vision is not something that must be created; it already exists in your body. You need to contact it. Your vision is the overall view of the expected results. It is an internal representation of your most important content; it is exciting, inspiring, convincing, and full of positive emotions. On the other hand, goals are specifically designed milestones, and if you are going to the end of the yellow brick road, you need to complete it. The disadvantage is that the goal does not necessarily inspire positive emotions. The goal is just a stepping stone on the road to the final destination.

A popular and effective way to set goals is to use the acronym SMART, which stands for specific (clear and accurate), measurable (you can quantify or measure progress), achievable (meaning reality), resources (you have the help you need). You don't need to rely on God's intervention (or others) and time (with start and end dates).

Why Meditation and Visualization Are Not the Same and How to Use Them

You will often hear that the terms meditation and visualization are used interchangeably. Still, they are not the same thing. Meditation and visualization hit the brain and body in entirely different ways. In the following, I will break down the differences and similarities and use each exercise to improve the quality of life:

When the Visualization Is Active, Meditation Is Quiet

There are many different meditation styles, but the class I teach is to let the body get adequate rest so that it can recover from stress. We sit quietly and let the assigned mantra do the work for us, effortlessly controlling our thoughts, breathing, or any other aspect of our experience. We have a theme: do less and do more. On the other hand, visualization is more active. We direct our breathing and thoughts in specific directions to achieve desired results, such as mentality sensation, or physical sensation. We use visualization to prepare our physical, mental, and emotional states for high performance enhanced immune function or better sleep.

Meditation Can Calm the Nervous System, and Visualization Can Reprogram It

Meditation can make the body rest even more profound than sleep, thereby exciting the nervous system. Rest can help the body recover from many things, including physical illness, but the most common is stress. Or, visualization can help us reprogram the old "fight or escape" stress response and help us enter the "keep and play" mindset. Fear affects breathing. First, so many of the visualization methods I use in the new thinking green course start with breathing work, then guide you through the introductory images, and usually end with a healthy posture (this is to make your body more confident, convenient exists).

Meditation Is Beyond Consciousness, and Visualization Requires You to Be Vigilant

Vedic meditation is the basis of my teaching. It can help you enter a verifiable fourth state of consciousness, which is different from awakening, sleeping, or dreaming. We went beyond the realm of thinking and entered the realm of existence. In contrast, visualization is more of a practice of wakefulness. When it happens, we will be more fully aware of it. We guide our ideas to visualize the best situation or use our imagination to have five sensory experiences of how your next high-demand situation works. Just as Olympic athletes use visualization before a competition to improve their performance, I recommend that you perform visualization before significant life events: public speeches, business negotiations, first dates, or any competition to relax and perform well.

Meditation Steps for Achieving Your Goals

This meditation will help you visualize your ideal work situation so that you can turn it into reality. "Work makes love visible." Like the following meditations, they have rich insights and practical exercises that can help you visualize your ideal work situation and turn it into reality. Please have a friend read this meditation to you, or record it, and play it to yourself. Read so that you can gain more in-depth wisdom and guidance.

Go In

Sit comfortably and close your eyes. Turn your attention to your breath, and when you exhale, imagine that the pressure will leave your body.

Visualization

From this deep phase of relaxation, imagine a place where you will feel comfortable, safe, and secure. Absorb the feeling of all areas. Breathing a peculiar smell and hearing sound. See it clearly as if you are focusing your camera on a huge image. There is a tunnel in the distance, made of branches, flowers or earth, and stones. Tunnels can help you understand yourself more deeply. Go through the tunnel and leave the everyday world behind.

On the other hand, see yourself in a "perfect" work environment. You don't have to try. Just stay open to impressions, insights, and feelings. It allows you to obtain information about your life work and the steps you need to highlight your life.

Appear

After about five minutes, return to the tunnel and rest at the other side's beautiful starting point. Shift your attention to breathing and body. Restore the excellent feeling of awakening consciousness. When you are available, open your eyes and write down what you have learned.

Understand Multi-Sensor Visualization

I use this easy-to-remember acronym to help me navigate through visualization files in a structured way:

- Kinesthetic
- Hearing
- Visual effects
- Sensual
- Conceptual

- Smell

- Taste

- Space

My imagination of the wind and warmth brought by sunlight gives people a physical feeling. I heard the waves. My imagination is not high, but I still get some spiritual pictures like the sun and blue sky. Then, I must remember the calm and peaceful mood of going to Toronto Lake, which always makes me deep in my heart. It's a bit tricky to use concepts to explain, but one of the simplest facts is that it is Lake Ontario and no other waters. It is also in Toronto, and I have a lot of history.

Next, I remembered the smell of water from the kettle that I used to bolt to the bike. I smelled the water and finally thought of the space element. I'm talking about the period of the bench. How thick must the wood be? It may sound stupid, but this is a way to deepen the visual meditation experience. Finally, I sometimes add some spatial factors, such as how long it takes to ride a bicycle on the lake and how the CN tower appears in the distance. When you practice them consistently, all these factors add up valuable.

Regular Meditation Locations and Time of Day

I have already mentioned my favorite meditation area at the moment. There are good reasons to believe that visiting the same place to meditate "anchoring" your practice. In this way, what I mean is that when arranging location etiquette, let your thoughts fall into practice. You can solve problems easily and quickly. Ultimately, you want to meditate anywhere, but by keeping a fixed time and place, you can develop in a bulletproof way faster than by constantly randomizing everything.

As they say, the failure of the plan is the failure of the project. There is especially great wisdom in taking full advantage of relaxation visualization. In my way, I don't get up in the morning without visualizing it first. In this way, when I will go for a walk and meditate, it is not so important anymore. However, I still have to make sure to keep the noontime.

Select an Object or Text

Powerful object-based meditation is the introduction to the airtight method. You draw a clock on the wall. The goal is to keep the clock in mind for as long as possible, up to 20 minutes. I don't think it's necessary to go so long. Even 2-5 minutes is sufficient. It doesn't have to be a timepiece either, mainly because such objects involve movement and sound (if there is a ticking sound). You can imagine vases, bookshelves, or toys that you had when you were a child.

I memorized the long, only started from the beginning, and only began to recite them in my mind when I was finished. Sometimes I will repeat them aloud, but usually, I do it silently. I used the Memory Palace, which provides the ultimate visual meditation because I will re-examine every part of my mental journey of laying out words.

Record Your Experience

I find out that keeping a journal is one of the best ways to learn more about meditation and how to deepen it. Although you can, of course, remember all the information about your experience, I think it's better to leave the memory for language learning, names, and other knowledge-based items. Just the day before, I was meditating in the morning. Suddenly, my father and brother had a vivid experience of a sleigh slip. I make sure to record it in the 5-year snapshot diary.

In this way, not only will I remember it, but I will return to my mind in handwritten form on the autopilot in a year. All of these do not require an app to remind me.

- Start in your area of life. Choose a place where you have been working hard or want to experience some transformation.

- Now, imagine that 6 to 12 months from now, you hope to live in this field the most possible. Imagine how you would imagine your life if all your hopes and dreams were realized. What is your ultimate reality? Try not to restrict limitations or negative emotions. Instead, get rid of your craziest desires.

- Next, connect with what you want to achieve in the next three months. Do it well. If the goal you choose is less important or meaningless, the result (even if you dare not achieve it) will not feel so special. Therefore, be sure to choose something big enough. Once you achieve this goal, you will have a high sense of accomplishment and will be full of motivation to set the next goal. Run the target through SMART acronyms to make sure it meets all appropriate conditions. Then, you are set!

- Now that you have achieved your goal, imagine your life after completing it. Create a picture or movie in your mind and enter the visual representation as if you are in it and looking through your own eyes. Adjust the quality of all sensory perceptions (taste, touch, sight, sound, smell) to create the most positive and authentic feeling. Who is with you? What happened around you?

- Next, jump out of the image you created, and then imagine floating in the air where you are now, carrying a mental picture with you. Take a deep breath, and when you exhale, use the breath to make the image full of vitality, full of positive energy and intention. Do this five times.

- Now is the time to imagine floating in the future and visually put the internal representation of your life's goal at the date and time set for achieving the goal.

- Pay attention to how all events between now and then re-evaluate yourself to support you in achieving your goals. Visualize this process to make it real.

- Once you feel good, go back to the present, close your eyes, and consider the steps you will take next week to bring yourself closer to your goal.

- Before opening your eyes, take a few deep breaths to ground yourself. Write down a list of your actions and record your experience.

- Finally, you must take action and stay focused. Every day, do something to bring you closer to achieving your goals and realizing your dreams.

Hypnosis to Improve Sleep Quality and Fall Asleep Instantly

We all know that sleep is an element part of a healthy lifestyle in addition to diet and exercise. Good quality sleep makes you feel alert during the day, vital to your health and well-being. However, getting a good night's sleep is easier said than done. If we don't have enough sleep for any reason, it will affect our behavior. Persistent poor sleep will bring many challenging side effects, and these side effects will affect all aspects of life.

Hypnotherapy is a popular method to solve deep-rooted sleep problems. It works by changing the way the previously programmed subconscious has learned to behave. All hypnosis comes from you. It is a state we enter every day, just before we fall asleep or just before waking up. In this case, your mind is more receptive. What is your subconscious hearing during sleep at this time?

The thing about the subconscious mind is that even if you don't feel it at all, it will always serve your benefit. Your mind thinks that you should fall asleep this way, so we need to tell you how you want to go now. Hypnotherapy has helped many people get rid of sleep disorders, sleep well, and benefit from new and improved sleep patterns. Hypnotherapy is a hypnotic drug with positive, beneficial effects. A qualified hypnotherapist (please make sure they are) can help you use this natural state faster, and more effectively to develop your subconscious mind to sleep well.

Even "trying to fall asleep" can affect your chances of falling asleep and staying asleep at the right time. When we "try," we immediately assume failure. Just think about when to lose weight or be on time. It is a hypnotherapist who uses techniques to induce relaxation and guide our subconscious mind to focus on what we want, thereby increasing our chances of getting and enjoying sleep.

Hypnosis may be reminiscent of images of people rattling like ducks on stage. Still, the reality is that it is usually more boring and induces sleep. Hypnotism may be a tool for some people who struggle with various sleep disorders, such as insomnia or sleepwalking. For people with insomnia, hypnosis can help relax the body and mind and eliminate the anxiety of falling asleep. On the other hand, a sleepwalker can learn to wake up when his feet fall on the ground through hypnotic advice. Hypnosis may also increase the time you spend in slow-wave sleep (deep sleep) by 80%. It is critical because deep sleep is essential for memory and recovery, so you will feel recovered when you wake up.

Contrary to what you might imagine, hypnosis does not occur by watching the pocket watch's swing. It is usually done by listening to verbal prompts from a hypnotherapist, which will put you in a like state, which can be compared to indulging in an excellent book to mediate your surroundings. For example, a meeting designed to help you sleep deeper may use words such as "relax," "deep," "relaxed," and "let go" to make a soft and soothing sound. Afterward, even while listening, you may have insomnia. Although some people describe hypnosis as being incredibly relaxing, your brain focuses on serious attention during hypnosis.

Hypnotherapy may be better for some people. That's because some people are more "understandable" than others—that is, they are more prone to hypnosis. However, about a quarter of people cannot be hypnotized. Are you interested in trying? People who use hypnotism to help solve sleep problems see results in just a few meetings, so you don't have to make a big commitment. Hypnotherapy is not an independent treatment for sleep disorders, but another tool that can be tried, and doctors, nurses, and psychotherapists usually practice it. Talk to your doctor about the referral.

What If I Cannot Sleep?

People with sleep disorders often use over-the-counter medicines and natural supplements (such as melatonin, valerian, and tryptophan) for self-treatment. Some people also turn to healthcare practitioners, most commonly doctors and psychiatrists. Doctors usually use drug interventions to treat sleep disorders. However, sleep medications called sedative-hypnotics or sleeping pills are not without risks. Long-term use of such drugs may cause dependence, daytime sleepiness, nausea, fatigue, confusion, and memory problems. Due to side effects, many people prefer non-drug therapies, including meditation, hypnosis, and sleep hygiene procedures. If you want to develop sleep quality, you first try the following methods:

- Maintain a consistent sleep and wake-up schedule.
- Enjoy a relaxing bedtime ceremony.
- Reduce nap.
- Exercise regularly.
- Avoid intense light and TV/computer before going to bed.
- Relax before going to bed and do activities that calm you down (reading, listening to soft music).
- Avoid eating at night, especially meals.
- Avoid alcohol, caffeine, and cigarettes before going to bed.

However, if these simple methods do not meet your needs, you may need to adopt a more comprehensive approach with a skilled sleep expert. According to scientific literature, cognitive behavioral therapy or CBT can effectively treat sleep disorders, mainly when used with hypnosis.

Hypnosis to Fall Asleep

Hypnotic intervention procedures are usually very flexible and should be customized and suitable for individual clients. Some of the available options that are valid include:

- The combination of hypnosis and other interventions (such as cognitive behavioral therapy, cognitive processing therapy, sleep hygiene),
- Self-hypnosis,
- Personal meeting with a hypnotherapist, and
- Group hypnosis meeting.

To treat insomnia, different hypnotic methods can be used. For example:

- A metaphor says that a fish goes deeper into the water and sleeps deeper,
- The age regression technology can encourage you to focus on the early memories of restorative sleep's easy arrival,

- Visualize the direction of relaxation (for example, relaxing scenes and sounds), and

- Self-reinforcing suggestions.

The benefit of hypnotizing to fall asleep is that successful interventions may be relatively short. It has been discovered that an average of 3 to 4 treatment courses may be sufficient to obtain the benefits of sleep results.

Family practice is usually encouraged in all types of meetings. For these users, you can use recordings, online resources, and other digital medical applications. In recent years, online applications such as Mindset have become powerful tools for self-hypnosis. The insomnia application makes sleep hypnotherapy more accessible and available to the public. Now, quality sleep is truly within reach.

Conclusion

Based on the above content, I concluded that hypnosis helps you to solve sleep problems. Adequate sleep is essential to help you to maintain optimal health and happiness. When you are awake, your body produces a chemical called adenosine, which accumulates throughout the day and eventually causes drowsiness, indicating you are ready to go to bed. Your sleep and daily relationship with wakefulness are controlled by two systems: your biological clock (or circadian rhythm) and sleep motivation.

Sleep keeps your heart healthy, prevents cancer, reduces stress, reduces inflammation, makes you more alert, improves your memory, helps you to lose weight, reduce the risk of depression, and helps the body repair itself. If you have lacked sleep, it may cause serious health risks. Long-term lack of sleep damages your mental health, reduces memory, makes weight loss more difficult, increase the risk of heart diseases, hypertension, stroke, diabetes, and lead to poor judgment. Insufficient sleep negatively affects your decision-making process and creativity, weakens the immune system, and cause skin aging.

The main reasons for not sleeping well include sleep apnea, diet, lack of exercise, pain, restless legs syndrome, depression, stress, poor sleep habits, Blu-ray insomnia, menopause insomnia, stealth caffeine insomnia, freedom insomnia, nap insomnia, and anxiety insomnia.

Insomnia is a sleeping disorder. It includes many sleep problems such as hard to sleep, wake up in the middle of the night, and restless sleep. Insomnia causes fatigue, irritability, excessive daytime sleepiness, causes weight gain, makes it difficult to lose weight, weakens the immune system, raises blood pressure level, chronic pain, and mental illness.

Cognitive-behavioral therapy for insomnia prevents you from falling asleep. It focuses on stimulus control and sleeps restriction. Establish a regular wake-up time, go to bed only when you are sleepy, don't lie awake in the ground, and avoid naps during the day are the basic principles of stimulus control.

You can control your sleep cycle through mindfulness meditation, mantra, yoga, exercise, and massage. The first step in improving sleep is to eat balanced, nutritious meals and snacks evenly throughout the day. For improving your sleep, skip sugar and caffeine, reaching complex carbohydrates, drink a soothing drink, boost your B vitamins, and drink milk. Before going to bed, you should avoid ice-cream, celery, pasta, pizza, candy bar, wine, and red meat.

Sleeping position will have a significant impact on waking up. The wrong way of sleeping (sleeping on the belly, freefall, starfish position, fetal position, log position) can cause aggravate neck or back pain. It can also block the airway to the lungs, causing problems such as obstructive apnea. People with congestive heart disease avoid sleeping on their back and left side. Sleeping on the right side can protect people with heart failure from further health damage.

If you face back pain, sleeping on your stomach or back may worsen the problem. You are switching to sleep on your side to minimize the risk of back pain. The best sleeping position for back pain is to lie on your back with your knees bent, use a pillow to lie on your side between your knees, sleep like a fetus, and sleep in front, with a pillow under your stomach. During pregnancy, try to sleep on the left side is often referred to as the ideal solution.

It would be best if you created an ideal sleeping environment by keeping the bedroom tidy, eliminating possible distractions, and organizing your room. Finding your perfect pillow, investing in a new mattress, cleaning up all the debris, and taking away all the electronic equipment also helps in the creation of the sleeping environment.

Better sleep habits directly change your physical and mental health. Unhealthy habits and lifestyle choices during the day will make you toss and turn at night, adversely affecting your mood, brain, heart health, immune system, creativity, vitality, and weight. You should keep your body's natural sleep-wake cycle, control your light exposure, and exercise during the day.

Positive Affirmations are some phrases (everything is fine, and I got support, or I believe everything is possible) that helps in improving the quality of sleep. The affirmation also enables you to find happiness, reduce anxiety and depression.

Hypnosis is a state similar to sleep. During hypnosis, you will enter in a more focused and attentive position. It is equivalent to daydreaming. It can be used to treat various diseases, conditions, and discomforts. It can also be applied to treat certain medical disorders, such as gastrointestinal diseases, skin diseases, or chronic pain. Sleep hypnosis involves listening to a hypnotherapist's verbal cues to bring you into a state with a suggested force. Hypnotherapists use different methods to induce relaxation, such as concentration, symptom control, and guided imaging.

Meditation trains us to reduce brainstorm and learn about current moments. Sleep meditation is a unique guided experience that alone provides natural sleep assistance, allowing us to let go of everything that happens, and everything said to relax while relaxing. During sleep-based meditation, you may discover new tools and techniques to help calm your mind and body, allowing you to relax and unwind.

Pay attention to body scans, visualization, gratitude, counting, silence, exercise-based meditation, and looking back at your day are some 'Guided Sleep Meditation Techniques.' Hypnotherapy is a popular method to solve deep-rooted sleep problems. It works by changing the way the previously programmed subconscious has learned to behave. All hypnosis comes from you. It is a state we enter every day, just before we fall asleep or just before waking up. In this case, your mind is more receptive.

Hypnotherapy is not an independent treatment for sleep disorders. But it is another tool that can be tried by doctors, nurses, and psychotherapists.

If you want to develop sleep quality, you first try to maintain a consistent wake-up schedule, reduce nap, exercise regularly, avoid intense light, avoid eating at night, especially meals, avoid alcohol, caffeine, and cigarettes before going to bed.

CPSIA information can be obtained
at www.ICGtesting.com
Printed in the USA
LVHW020750061120
670809LV00004B/441